How to Use This Book

Look for these special features in this book:

SIDEBARS, **CHARTS**, **GRAPHS**, and original **MAPS** expand your understanding of what's being discussed—and also make useful sources for classroom reports.

FAQs answer common **F**requently **A**sked **Q**uestions about people, places, and things.

WOW FACTORS offer "Who knew?" facts to keep you thinking.

TRAVEL GUIDE gives you tips on exploring the state—either in person or right from your chair!

PROJECT ROOM provides fun ideas for school assignments and incredible research projects. Plus, there's a guide to primary sources—what they are and how to cite them.

Please note: All statistics are as up-to-date as possible at the time of publication. Population data is taken from the 2010 census.

Consultants: Rex Buchanan, Associate Director for Public Outreach, Kansas Geological Survey; Virgil Dean, Historian and Editor, Kansas Historical Society; William Loren Katz

Book production by The Design Lab

Library of Congress Cataloging-in-Publication Data
Cannarella, Deborah.
Kansas / by Deborah Cannarella. — Revised edition.
pages cm. — (America the beautiful, third series)
Includes bibliographical references and index.
Audience: Ages 9–12.
ISBN 978-0-531-28280-9 (lib. bdg.)
1. Kansas—Juvenile literature. I. Title.
F681.3.C26 2014
978.1—dc23   2013044321

©2015, 2009 Scholastic Inc.
All rights reserved. Published in 2015 by Children's Press, an imprint of Scholastic Inc.
Printed in the United States of America 141
SCHOLASTIC, CHILDREN'S PRESS, and associated logos are trademarks and/or registered trademarks of Scholastic Inc.

2 3 4 5 6 7 8 9 10 R 24 23 22 21 20 19 18 17 16 15

AMERICA ★ THE ★ BEAUTIFUL

Kansas

BY DEBORAH CANNARELLA

Third Series, Revised Edition

Children's Press®
An Imprint of Scholastic Inc.
New York ★ Toronto ★ London ★ Auckland ★ Sydney
Mexico City ★ New Delhi ★ Hong Kong
Danbury, Connecticut

CONTENTS

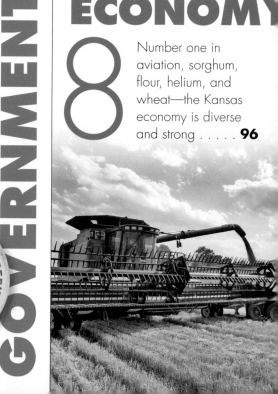

GROWTH AND CHANGE

4

FREE STATE CONVENTION!

All persons who are favorable to a union of effort, and a permanent organization of all the Free State elements of Kansas Territory, and who wish to secure upon the broadest platform the co-operation of all who agree upon this point, are requested to meet at their several places of holding elections, in their respective districts on the 25th of August, instant, at one o'clock, P. M., and appoint five delegates to each representative to which they were entitled in the Legislative Assembly, who shall meet in general Convention at

Big Springs, Wednesday, Sept. 5th '55,

at 10 o'clock A. M., for the purpose of adopting a Platform upon which all may act harmoniously who prefer Freedom to Slavery. The nomination of a Delegate to Congress, will also come up before the General Convention. Union and harmony are absolutely necessary to success. Let no sectional or party issues distract or prevent the perfect co-operation of Free State men. And to contend against them successfully, we also must be united.— pro-slavery party are fully and effectually organized. No jars nor minor issues divide them. Let every man then do his duty and we are certain of victory. Without prudence and harmony of action we are certain to fail. Let every man then do his immediate and effective steps to insure a full and correct representation for every District in the Territory, without distinction, are earnestly requested to take immediate and effective steps to insure a full and correct representation of the Mass Convention in session at Lawrence.

All Free State men, without distinction, "United we stand; divided we fall."

By order of the Executive Committee of the Free State Party of the Territory of Kansas, as per resolution of the Mass Convention in session at Lawrence.

Aug 15th and 16th, 1855.

J. K. GOODIN, Sec'y.

C. ROBINSON, Chairman.

Herald of Freedom, Print.

MORE MODERN TIMES

5

9 TRAVEL GUIDE

PROJECT ROOM

★

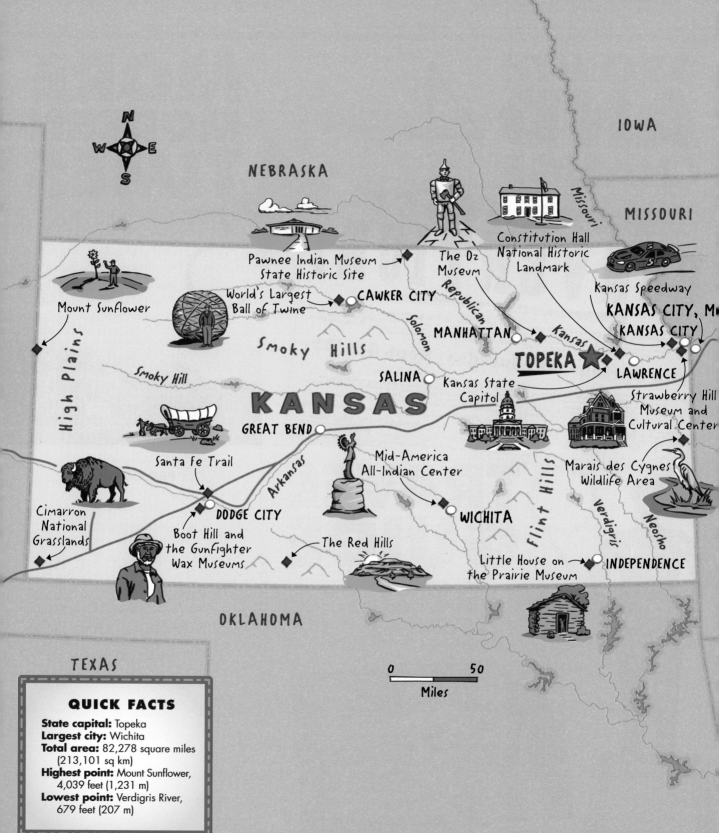

IOWA

NEBRASKA

MISSOURI

Pawnee Indian Museum
State Historic Site

The Oz
Museum

Constitution Hall
National Historic
Landmark

Kansas Speedway

Mount Sunflower

World's Largest
Ball of Twine

CAWKER CITY

KANSAS CITY, M

KANSAS CITY

High Plains

Smoky Hills

MANHATTAN

Kansas

Smoky Hill

KANSAS

SALINA

TOPEKA

LAWRENCE

Kansas State
Capitol

Strawberry Hill
Museum and
Cultural Center

GREAT BEND

Santa Fe Trail

Mid-America
All-Indian Center

Marais des Cygnes
Wildlife Area

Arkansas

Flint Hills

Verdigris

Neosho

Cimarron
National
Grasslands

DODGE CITY

Boot Hill and
the Gunfighter
Wax Museums

The Red Hills

WICHITA

Little House on
the Prairie Museum

INDEPENDENCE

OKLAHOMA

TEXAS

0   50
Miles

QUICK FACTS

State capital: Topeka
Largest city: Wichita
Total area: 82,278 square miles
(213,101 sq km)
Highest point: Mount Sunflower,
4,039 feet (1,231 m)
Lowest point: Verdigris River,
679 feet (207 m)

Welcome to Kansas!

HOW DID KANSAS GET ITS NAME?

Beginning in the 16th century, many European explorers visited the region that is now Kansas. There they met Native Americans who called themselves by a name that the explorers thought sounded like "Kansa" or "Kanza." Over the years, explorers wrote the name in many different ways—"Konza," "Canses," "Kansez," and "Kanzas." Some shortened the word to "Kaw," which is what these Native Americans are sometimes called today. When the region became a state, its name was spelled "Kansas." In the language of the Kaw people, the name means "wind people" or "people of the south wind."

8

READ ABOUT

A sunflower field
at sunset

CHAPTER ONE

LAND

★

KANSAS LIES IN THE GREAT PLAINS REGION OF THE UNITED STATES, BUT THERE'S NOTHING PLAIN ABOUT IT! Rolling prairie, rugged hills, eerie chalk formations, and even sand dunes fill its 82,278 square miles (213,101 square kilometers). The land rises gently from the state's lowest point, 679 feet (207 meters) along the Verdigris River in the southeastern corner, to its highest point, 4,039 feet (1,231 m) on Mount Sunflower in the far west.

State Geo-Facts

Along with the state's geographical highlights, this chart ranks Kansas's land, water, and total area compared to all other states.

Total area; rank . . .82,278 square miles (213,101 sq km); 15th
Land; rank. . . . .81,762 square miles (211,764 sq km); 13th
Water; rank . . . . . . .516 square miles (1,336 sq km); 42nd
Inland water; rank. . 516 square miles (1,336 sq km); 35th
Geographic center . . . . . Rice County, about 1.5 miles (2.4 km) southeast of Bushton
Latitude . . . . 37° N to 40° N
Longitude . . . . 94°38' W to 102°1'34" W
Highest point . . . . Mount Sunflower, 4,039 feet (1,231 m)
Lowest point . . . . Verdigris River, 679 feet (207 m)
Largest city . . . . Wichita
Longest river . . . . Arkansas River

Source: U.S. Census Bureau, 2010 census

The smallest state, Rhode Island, could fit inside Kansas 53 times!

These fossils of crinoids, which are marine animals also known as sea lilies, were found in the Niobrara formation in western Kansas.

MIDWAY, USA

Kansas is, as the people who live there might say, "smack dab" in the center of the country. One of the state's many nicknames is "Midway, USA." In fact, the exact center of the contiguous United States (all the states but Alaska and Hawai'i) is located in Kansas.

The state is an almost perfect rectangle, with the upper right corner nibbled away by the path of the Missouri River. Kansas is almost twice as wide from west to east as it is from north to south. It is bordered by Missouri on the east, Colorado on the west, Nebraska on the north, and Oklahoma on the south.

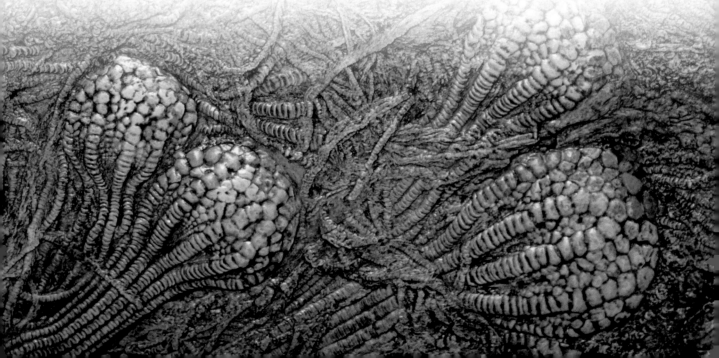

OCEANS AND ICE

Ancient events shaped the land that is now Kansas. More than 65 million years ago, much of what is now Kansas was at the bottom of the sea. This fact is hard to believe when you consider that Kansas is 1,265 miles (2,036 km) away from the Pacific Ocean, 1,342 miles (2,160 km) away from the Atlantic Ocean, and 600 miles (966 km) from any other large body of water. Sand, gravel, plants, and animals in ancient seas settled to the bottom. Over time, these materials turned into **sedimentary** rock, such as chalk, limestone, and shale. Scientists have found many **fossils** of ancient fish, reptiles, and birds in the state's chalk beds.

The landscape of Kansas has also been shaped by ice. Over hundreds of thousands of years, several **glaciers** moved across much of North America and then retreated again. The Kansan glacier covered what is now the northeastern part of the state about 600,000 years ago. It carried rock, gravel, sand, and clay along with it, scraping the surface of the land below. When the ice melted, some of this material was left behind. It formed a rich soil called till.

LAND REGIONS

Kansas can be divided into three major regions. The Great Plains region lies in the west. The Dissected Till Plains region and the Southeastern Plains are both in the east.

MINI-BIO

LEWIS LINDSAY DYCHE: NATURALIST

Lewis Lindsay Dyche (1857–1915) was a man of many talents: professor, environmentalist, explorer, game warden, and showman. As a child, he learned about nature by hunting, trapping, and fishing. While attending college in Emporia, Kansas, he went on expeditions to collect mammals and plants from local regions. Dyche learned taxidermy, the art of stuffing animals for display, and used it to show off the specimens he gathered. He later made 23 expeditions to Greenland, where he continued his work as a hunter and an explorer.

? **Want to know more?** Visit www.facts fornow.scholastic.com and enter the keyword **Kansas**.

WORDS TO KNOW

sedimentary *formed from clay, sand, and gravel that settled at the bottom of a body of water*

fossils *the remains or prints of ancient animals or plants left in stone*

glaciers *slow-moving masses of ice*

Blooming yucca plants in the Smoky Hills

Q8 HOW IS "ARKANSAS RIVER" PRONOUNCED?

A8 It depends on where you live. The people of Kansas call this river the "ar-KAN-zus," pronouncing the end of it the same as they pronounce "Kansas." People in the state of Arkansas pronounce the river's name "AR-kun-saw," just like their state's name.

Great Plains

The Great Plains region covers the western two-thirds of Kansas. The western half of this region is called the High Plains. The eastern half is called the High Plains Border.

The Great Plains region is dry and flat, with few trees. The short grasses that grow on the open prairies are full of nutrients, making them the perfect food for the cattle raised on the many ranches in the area. This part of Kansas is flat, but it has the highest elevation in the state. Mount Sunflower rises to 4,039 feet (1,231 m) along the western border. The Smoky Hills—named for the morning haze that gathers in the valley—lie in the High Plains Border region.

The Arkansas River flows through the southern part of the Great Plains region. The river begins in Colorado and winds its way to Arkansas. Sand dunes rise along the Cimarron and Arkansas rivers. These dunes formed in the last several thousand years, as sand blew out of the river channels. Tall chalk formations such as Monument Rocks and Castle Rock also rise in the Great Plains.

HEALING HILLS

The Red Hills lie in the Great Plains near the Oklahoma border. What gives the hills their orange-red color? Iron oxide, the mineral we know as rust. The Plains Indians called these hills the "Medicine Hills." They believed that spirits who lived in the region's springs and streams helped cure sicknesses. In fact, these waters contain natural salts that help fight infection and heal cuts more quickly.

The government made most of the 150 lakes in Kansas to help control flooding, for recreation, and to provide water for drinking and watering crops. Milford Lake, on the Republican River in the High Plains Border, is the largest lake in the state. It has 163 miles (262 km) of shoreline.

The Cheyenne Bottoms, also in the High Plains Border, is the largest marshland in the interior of the United States. Almost half of the shorebirds in North America stop there during their spring **migration**. More than 320 species—including whooping cranes and sandhill cranes—have visited the spot.

SEE IT HERE!

BIG BASIN

Dips in the earth's surface mark the High Plains of Kansas. These dips are called sinkholes, or sinks. Thousands of years ago, beds of salt and gypsum (a soft mineral) that lay several hundred feet below the earth's surface dissolved. The land above them collapsed, creating sinkholes. Big Basin, a sinkhole in southern Kansas, is about 1 mile (1.6 km) across and more than 100 feet (30 m) deep.

WORD TO KNOW

migration *movement from one place to another*

Sandhill crane in flight

Dissected Till Plains

About 600,000 years ago, huge glaciers moved across north-eastern Kansas, leaving behind a layer of rich, black soil. The glaciers also carried large boulders from places as far away as today's South Dakota, Iowa, and Minnesota.

The rocky and hilly northeast is full of woods and streams. The Big Blue, Kansas, and Missouri rivers form the natural borders of this region. The Big Blue River combines with the Smoky Hill and Republican rivers to form the Kansas River, which flows from Junction City to Kansas City. The Kansas River, also known as the Kaw River, is one of the most important rivers in the state. It provides drinking water and a place of recreation for the many people who live in the northeast. It joins the Missouri River at the state border.

This waterfall is part of the Elk River, near the town of Elk Falls.

Kansas Topography

Use the color-coded elevation chart to see on the map Kansas's high points (orange) and low points (green). Elevation is measured as the distance above or below sea level.

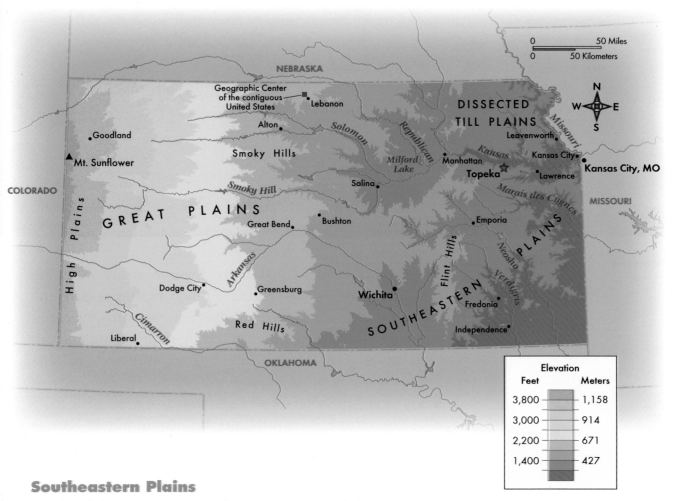

Elevation	
Feet	Meters
3,800	1,158
3,000	914
2,200	671
1,400	427

Southeastern Plains

South of the Kansas River lies the Osage Plains, an area that extends into three other states. The rich prairie land was once covered in tall grasses. In some places, flat-topped hills with gently sloping sides rise from the land. **Geologists** call these land formations cuestas, the Spanish word for "hill" or "cliff."

WORD TO KNOW

geologists *scientists who study the history of Earth*

Cattle grazing in the Flint Hills

The Flint Hills are the largest remaining area of tallgrass prairie in North America.

The Marais des Cygnes River is one of several rivers that flow through this region. French explorers gave the river its name, which means "marsh of the swans," because so many swans stopped here during their spring and fall migrations. The Marais des Cygnes National Wildlife Refuge is still home to many types of birds. It also contains the largest hardwood forest in Kansas.

The Flint Hills stretch north to south across Kansas and extend into Nebraska and Oklahoma. The hills are named for the flint found in the soil. Flint is a type of rock that early Native people sometimes shaped to form tools. The gently rolling Flint Hills are often compared to a sea of grass. The hills support many types of native grasses. Tall grasses once blanketed much of central North America. Today, the Tallgrass Prairie National Preserve in the Flint Hills is one of the few places where visitors can experience the tallgrass prairie as it once was.

The rugged Ozark Plateau, which extends into Arkansas, Missouri, and Oklahoma, is very different from the rest of Kansas. The hilly Ozarks contain the oldest rocks in the state. These limestone rocks date back hundreds of millions of years! Limestone erodes easily, so there are many caves throughout the region. Oak and hickory trees grow in the rocky soil, but unlike most of Kansas, the land in the Ozarks is not good farmland.

Weather Report

This chart shows record temperatures (high and low) for the state, as well as average temperatures (July and January) and average annual precipitation

Record high temperature . . . . 121°F (49°C) at Fredonia on July 18, 1936, and at Alton on July 24, 1936
Record low temperature . . . . −40°F (−40°C) at Lebanon on February 13, 1905
Average July temperature, Wichita . . . . .81°F (27°C)
Average January temperature, Wichita . . . . .32°F (0°C)
Average annual precipitation, Wichita . . . . 33 inches (84 cm)

Source: National Climatic Data Center, NESDIS, NOAA, U.S. Department of Commerce

EXTREMES OF WEATHER

Kansas is one of the sunniest states in the nation. It is also unusually windy. In fact, Dodge City, in the southwest part of the state, is the windiest city in the United States. Flat and treeless, it sits without protection from the powerful winds that sweep across the Great Plains. During the dry winter and early spring, strong winds in western Kansas can pick up the soil and carry it away, damaging crops and sometimes producing dangerous dust storms.

Southeastern Kansas is the rainiest part of the state. The southwestern region has frequent dry spells, called droughts.

In Kansas, severe storms can develop suddenly. Blizzards dump snow in the winter, and summer thunderstorms produce heavy rain, hail, and—sometimes—tornadoes. Kansas lies in Tornado Alley, an area that stretches from Texas through parts of Oklahoma, Kansas, and Nebraska. More tornadoes tear through this region than anywhere else in the country.

In an average year, around 50 tornadoes strike Kansas.

TORNADO TROUBLE

A tornado is a powerful, swirling column of air that spins across land or water at great speed. Most tornadoes are formed in the thunderclouds of large, violent storms called supercells.

Warm, moist air close to the ground rises above cooler, drier air to create an updraft within the storm. The warm air then forms rain or hail, which creates a downdraft. As the winds change direction and speed, the updraft and downdraft form a spinning column. If the column turns so that one end touches the ground, it becomes a tornado. As the tornado travels, that end stays in contact with the ground. The other end forms into a large, often funnel-shaped cloud, sometimes thousands of feet high.

Wind speeds in tornadoes sometimes reach 300 miles (483 km) per hour—strong enough to lift buildings right off the ground. The United States, especially the Great Plains region, has more tornadoes than any other place in the world. When the cool air from Canada meets the warm air from the Gulf of Mexico, conditions are right to start tornado trouble.

On May 4, 2007, a powerful tornado hit the town of Greensburg. Winds inside the tornado reached speeds greater than 200 miles (322 km) per hour. The wedge tornado (named for its shape) measured almost 2 miles (3.2 km) wide and traveled along the ground for more than 20 miles (32 km). In about 30 minutes, 95 percent of Greensburg was destroyed, and 11 people were killed. The National Weather Service set off a warning siren in Dodge City 20 minutes before the tornado hit, which saved many lives.

When it came time to rebuild the devastated town, residents and city officials decided to "go green." They would build a town that uses renewable energy sources, such as wind and solar power. All city-owned buildings were rebuilt to meet strict energy-saving standards. Private business owners and homeowners also rebuilt to improve the energy performance of their buildings. Today, Greensburg is a model community of green energy.

A tornado descends upon the plains near El Dorado.

Kansas's National Park Areas

This map shows some of Kansas's national parks, monuments, preserves, and other areas protected by the National Park Service.

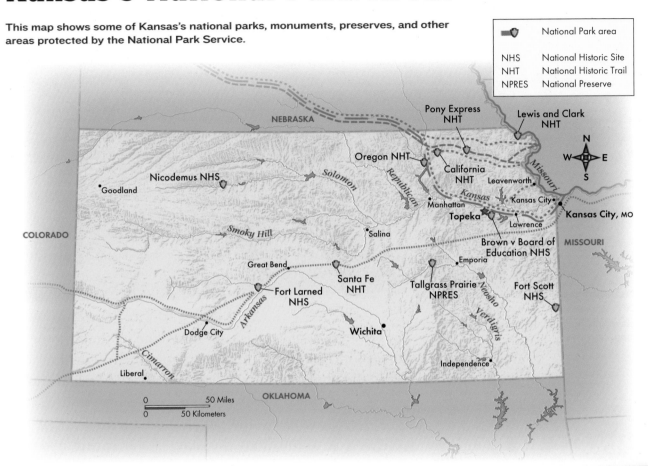

	National Park area
NHS	National Historic Site
NHT	National Historic Trail
NPRES	National Preserve

ANIMAL LIFE

True to the words of "Home on the Range"—the state song—Kansas is where "the deer and the antelope play." You'll also find plenty of elk, rabbits, coyotes, and raccoons, along with 14 species of lizards and several species of bats. In the High Plains, prairie dogs live in underground towns that often stretch across dozens of acres. Above the ground in Kansas, you'll see American buffalo, or bison, grazing in parks and on ranches.

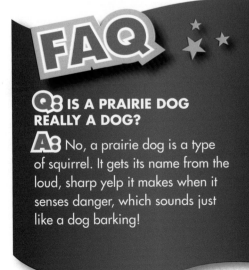

FAQ

Q: IS A PRAIRIE DOG REALLY A DOG?

A: No, a prairie dog is a type of squirrel. It gets its name from the loud, sharp yelp it makes when it senses danger, which sounds just like a dog barking!

Many wild turkeys make their home in Kansas.

Hundreds of species of birds make their home in Kansas, including the American goldfinch, the American robin, the blue jay, and the western meadowlark, the state bird. Pheasants live in western and central Kansas, and quails and turkeys are found throughout the state. Each spring and fall, many birds travel through Kansas as they migrate. The Marais des Cygnes National Wildlife Refuge is home to many bird species, including the endangered peregrine falcon.

ANIMALS IN DANGER

As humans clear more and more of the Kansas prairie to create farms, roads, and buildings, the animals that once lived there disappear. Prairie chickens nest, hide, and eat in the protective cover of the state's native grasses and shrubs. They particularly like sand sagebrush and the little bluestem grasses that grow in southwestern Kansas. The state has asked private landowners to keep areas planted with grasses and shrubs so that these animals have a place to live.

Another animal that needs the state's protection is the eastern spotted skunk. This little creature—which has dotted white stripes on its black fur—lives at the edges of wooded areas and near rocks and shrubs in the prairie grasslands. It also likes farm buildings, where it can easily find food and shelter.

Greater prairie chicken

Kansas has the largest population of prairie chickens in North America. Greater prairie chickens live in the northern and eastern grasslands, especially in the Flint Hills. Lesser prairie chickens live in the short grass and prairies of the southwest, especially in the Red Hills and Cimarron National Grasslands.

PLANT LIFE

Kansas is nicknamed the Sunflower State for a very good reason. Many varieties of sunflowers grow in Kansas. In September, the fields and roadsides are full of these tall yellow flowers. The sunflowers also attract butterflies—a beautiful sight to see!

Hundreds of other types of wildflowers dot the Kansas landscape. In spring and summer, wild daisy, clover, compass plant, butterfly milkweed, coneflower, and Indian blanket flower fill the prairies.

Native grasses cover about one-third of the state. These grasses protect the soil from washing away in the rain or blowing away in the wind. They also serve as food for grazing cattle and other animals. Not all the grass in Kansas is alike. There are about 200 varieties of native grass. Big

The tallest sunflower ever measured rose 27 feet (8.2 m) high—about as tall as a two-story house! It was grown in Germany.

A field of sunflowers in western Kansas

bluestem and little bluestem grow in almost every part of the state. Buffalo grass is also native to the state.

The cottonwood is the state tree. It's a relative of the willow and grows along lakes, streams, and rivers. The cottonwood does not live long—only about 70 years—but the tree grows fast, about 8 feet (2.4 m) per year. The cottonwood is sometimes called the Pioneer Tree because early settlers used it for shade, fuel, and building material. Eastern Kansas has many types of hardwood trees. Black walnut trees, valuable for their wood and nuts, grow in southeastern Kansas.

Hikers stop for a rest in the Konza Prairie.

A Kansas farmer plants wheat in a dry field.

PRECIOUS WATER

Kansas has few natural sources of water. The western part of the state is especially dry and prone to drought. This region relies on the Ogallala Aquifer as a source of water for drinking, washing, farming, and industry. An aquifer is a sandy underground formation that holds water, just like a sponge. The Ogallala Aquifer lies beneath eight states in the Great Plains, extending from South Dakota to Texas.

Experts believe that 69 percent of the aquifer will be used by 2060. It is replenished with rainfall and runoff from the ground—but not fast enough. In 2006, water levels in western Kansas hit new lows. These levels broke records set during the worst droughts in Kansas's history.

To address this problem, the state is working with the U.S. Department of Agriculture to encourage farmers to conserve more water. One idea is to convert more land to dryland farming. This farming method, which has long been practiced in the region, does not require **irrigation**. Winter wheat and sorghum, two of Kansas's most successful crops, are well suited to dryland farming. Another idea is to pay farmers not to grow as many crops. Instead, they would let native trees and grasses grow on some of their farmland.

WORD TO KNOW

irrigation *watering land by artificial means to promote plant growth*

READ ABOUT

Archaeologist Bob
Thompson sifts
through Native
artifacts near
Lindsborg.

c.10,000 BCE

Paleo-Indians hunt
on the Great Plains

8000 BCE

Large animals such
as mammoths and
mastodons die out in
what is now Kansas

6000 BCE ▲

Archaic people in what
is now Kansas develop
stone tools for hunting
and grinding seeds

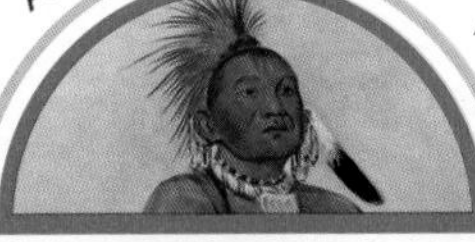

CHAPTER TWO

FIRST PEOPLE

★

BENEATH THE TALLGRASSES AND ROLLING HILLS OF KANSAS, YOU CAN STILL FIND EVIDENCE OF THE EARLY PEOPLE WHO ONCE LIVED THERE. Tools, pottery, bones, and weapons made thousands of years ago have been discovered throughout the state. Early Kansans also carved pictures into the soft sandstone cliffs in the central part of the state.

100 CE

Clay pottery becomes common

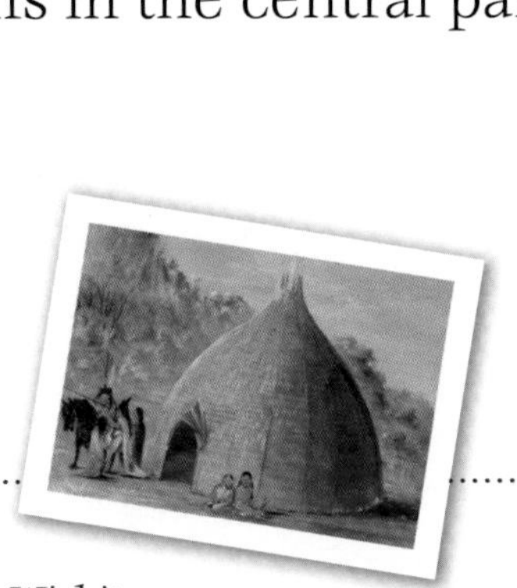

1500s ▸

Kansa, Pawnee, Wichita (right), Osage, and other groups live in the region

Early people hunted mammoths and other large game with spears.

WORD TO KNOW

extinct *no longer existing*

THE ANCIENT PEOPLE

People first moved across the Great Plains region of North America some 11,000 to 12,000 years ago. These people, called Paleo-Indians, roamed the wide-open plains in search of food. They hunted large, long-horned bison, a relative of the American buffalo. They also hunted other now-**extinct** animals, such as mastodons and mammoths, relatives of the modern-day elephant.

When the herds of animals moved, the people followed. They traveled across the plains on foot, living in temporary shelters. They made their clothes from animal skins. They made tools from animal bones. In addition to meat, the Paleo-Indians ate berries, seeds, and roots.

Slowly, over a few thousand years, the climate grew warmer and drier, and many of the large mammals became extinct. People began to hunt smaller animals such as deer and rabbits. They also began eating a wider variety of plants.

The Archaic culture developed by about 6000 BCE. Because they were no longer following large herds, people did not need to travel as much. Archaic people developed stone tools for hunting and for grinding seeds to make food. The Flint Hills region of Kansas is filled with chert, or flint, the mineral that they shaped into tools and spear points.

BUILDING VILLAGES

Kansas's people eventually began to settle in more permanent villages. There they grew corn, squash, and beans. From time to time, they left their villages to hunt the buffalo, deer, and other animals that roamed the plains. They hunted with bows and arrows instead of spears. Clay pots became common throughout Kansas by about 100 CE.

Spear points made of flint

By around 1500 CE, some people in Kansas lived in earth lodges. These round homes were made of wood and covered with willow branches and **sod**. When the grass on the sod grew, the lodge looked like a small hill, hidden in the landscape.

Other people lived in cone-shaped grass houses that looked like beehives. In the center of the roof was a small hole, which allowed smoke from the cooking fire inside the house to escape.

WORD TO KNOW

sod *soil thickly packed together with grass and roots*

Native American Peoples
(Before European Contact)

This map shows the general area of Native American peoples before European settlers arrived.

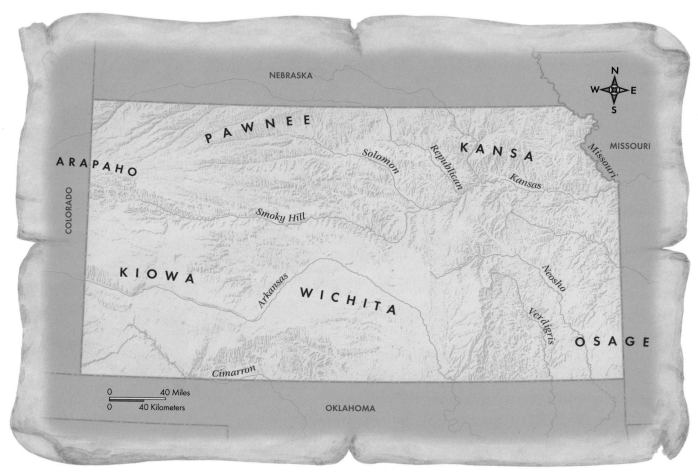

THE KANSA PEOPLE

By the time Europeans first arrived in the 1500s, several different cultures were thriving in the region. The Kansa, or Kaw, nation gave their name to the future state. The word Kansa means "wind people" or "people of the south wind." The Kansa people believed that the wind and all other forces of nature were sacred.

At one time the Kansa people lived on land that stretched across what is now northern Kansas and into Missouri. In Kansa villages, multiple families often lived together in one large circular or oval lodge. These dwellings had wood frames and were covered with mats of grass or bark. The Kansa people grew corn, beans, and other crops. They also hunted bison.

In summer and fall, the Kansa people formed hunting groups and left the village. They carried portable homes, called tepees, which they made from animal skins. Each group chose leaders who were in charge and kept the peace. When the hunters returned to the village, the leaders shared the meat with them as payment for their work.

A group of Kansa men performing a dance inside a village lodge

Picture Yourself . . .

Coming of Age in a Kansa Village

You are a Kansa boy, 12 or 13 years old. It is time to begin your life as a man. To do this, you must travel alone on a vision quest. You head into the wilderness, living on your own for several days. During this time, you eat no food and drink no water. Instead, you wait to have a special dream, a dream about warriors in your family, or about bears, buffalo, or other animals. After the dream, you return to the village and tell your family and others about it. They give you a new name based on the meaning of your dream. From that day on, you are considered an adult.

WORD TO KNOW

breechcloths *garments worn by men over their lower bodies*

Kansa women planted and harvested corn, beans, potatoes, squash, and pumpkins. They also gathered nuts, roots, and berries. The women raised the children and cooked the meals. They sometimes traveled with the men on buffalo hunts, to dry the meat and prepare the animal skins.

Kansa men wore **breechcloths** around their waists. They also wore deerskin leggings and soft shoes called moccasins. The moccasins were made of deer, elk, or buffalo skin.

The men removed all the hair from their arms, chins, and eyebrows. They also plucked the hair from their heads, leaving only a narrow strip from top to back. The men sometimes painted this strip of hair orange-red with a natural dye. Others decorated their hair with eagle feathers or deer tails. The men also wore earrings made of beads, shell, or other materials. Some of them wore strands of bear claws around their necks or legs. Many people had tattoos.

Kansa women wore wraparound skirts and shawls. They made their clothes, blankets, and shoes from animal skins. They decorated the skins with porcupine quills that were dyed different colors (red, black, or yellow) and stitched in decorative patterns onto pipes, bags, and medicine bundles.

THE OSAGE PEOPLE

The Osage people lived in villages along the Missouri River. They also settled along the Osage River in western Missouri, the Little Osage and Neosho rivers in southeastern Kansas, and the Arkansas River into Oklahoma and Arkansas. Painter George Catlin visited Kansas in 1835 and described Osage men as the tallest people in North America. Osage men stood around 6 feet (183 cm) tall on average.

Osages had much in common with the Kansa people. They grew corn, beans, and pumpkins in their villages. They also hunted buffalo. In spring, they left their villages for the summer hunt and returned near the end of summer to harvest their crops. In September, they left to hunt again and returned in winter.

FAQ

Q8 WHAT IS A MEDICINE BUNDLE?

A8 A medicine bundle is a pouch made of animal skin. It contains beads, bones, stones, feathers, or other small objects with special meaning. The Plains Indians believed that medicine bundles had special powers that protected their families and tribes.

This painting by George Catlin depicts three Osage men.

BLACKBEAR BOSIN: NATIVE AMERICAN ARTIST

Francis Blackbear Bosin (1921–1980) was named after his father's father, a Kiowa leader. His mother was Comanche. Bosin was born in Oklahoma and moved to Wichita in 1940. He began painting as a child and eventually began working as an illustrator. Although he was primarily a painter, Bosin created one piece of sculpture. *Keeper of the Plains* (above) is a 44-foot-tall (13 m) steel statue of a Native American. It stands on a large stone in downtown Wichita, where the Arkansas and Little Arkansas rivers meet.

? Want to know more? Visit www.factsfornow .scholastic.com and enter the keyword **Kansas**.

Osage communities were divided into two groups—the People of the Sky and the People of the Land. They believed that a great power had created these two groups. Their villages had a main road that ran east to west. The People of the Sky lived on the north side of the road, and the People of the Land lived on the south side.

THE PAWNEE PEOPLE

The Pawnee people lived in the area that now extends from north-central Kansas to central Nebraska.

The Pawnee language is called Caddo. In their language, the Pawnee people called themselves "men of men." Europeans gave them the name Pawnee, which may come from the Caddo word for horn. Some experts believe that the Pawnee may have been given this name because of the unique hairstyle worn by Pawnee men. These men shaved their heads except for a single lock that was combed to stick up like a horn.

THE WICHITA PEOPLE

Like Pawnees, the Wichita people spoke the Caddo language. Wichitas called themselves Kitikitish, a word that means "raccoon eyelids." Their name describes the tattoos that both the men and women had on their faces and eyelids, which created dark patterns.

W★W

Plains Indians developed a sign language. Members of different Native American nations "spoke" in sign language to communicate with one another.

Wichitas lived in round grass houses. The houses are sometimes called wikiups or wigwams. The house frame was made of several poles that were bent and tied together and then covered with layers of long prairie grass. A hole at the top let smoke escape from the cooking fire. Doors at the front and back allowed breezes to pass through to cool the house. Beds were raised off the floor on posts.

Wichitas lived along the Arkansas River in south-central Kansas. One day, a group of strangers entered one of the Wichita villages. They spoke an unknown language and rode on beasts never seen before. These Spanish newcomers didn't stay long, but in time, contact with other Europeans would change the world of the Native Americans forever.

Wichita homes, as shown in this George Catlin painting, were often thatched with prairie grass.

READ ABOUT

Francisco Vásquez de
Coronado exploring
North America

1541

Spanish explorer
Francisco Vásquez de
Coronado enters what
is now Kansas

1673

French explorers Louis
Jolliet and Jacques
Marquette draw the first
maps to show parts of
Kansas

1682 ▶

French explorer René-
Robert Cavelier, Sieur
de La Salle, claims
Louisiana, which includes
Kansas, for France

CHAPTER THREE

EXPLORATION AND SETTLEMENT

★

IN FEBRUARY 1540, FRANCISCO VÁSQUEZ DE CORONADO LED A PARTY OF MORE THAN 1,000 SPANISH SOLDIERS AND INDIANS NORTH OUT OF MEXICO CITY. They were searching for the legendary Seven Cities of Gold. By the spring of 1541, Coronado had trekked all the way to what is now Kansas. He never found gold, but he did visit a Wichita village.

c.1700 ▶

Native Americans on the Great Plains acquire horses

1744

Fort de Cavagnial becomes the first European settlement in Kansas

1762

France gives Louisiana to Spain

SEE IT HERE!

EL CUARTELEJO

In Lake Scott State Park, you'll find the remains of the only known Indian **pueblo** in Kansas. The Spanish rulers of New Mexico mistreated the Native people. In 1664, a group of Taos people fled to what is now western Kansas to escape the harsh treatment. Their village became known as El Cuartelejo. The Indians built pueblo dwellings like those they had left behind in New Mexico. They also grew crops and built canals to redirect spring water, creating what may have been the first irrigation system in Kansas. Today, the remains of this pueblo are a national historic landmark.

WORD TO KNOW

pueblo *a flat-roofed house, usually made from dried mud and straw, built by Native Americans of the desert Southwest; also, a community of these houses*

CLAIMED FOR SPAIN

Coronado later wrote that Kansas was home to the best soil he had seen "for producing all the products of Spain." He wrote about "prunes like those of Spain," nuts, sweet grapes, and mulberries. Coronado claimed the land for Spain, but it would be more than a century before Europeans returned to Kansas.

THE ARRIVAL OF THE FRENCH

In 1673, a French Canadian trader named Louis Jolliet traveled with Father Jacques Marquette down the Mississippi River into what is now Arkansas. Although they prob-

Two oarsmen row Father Jacques Marquette's boat on the Mississippi River.

Exploration of Kansas

The colored arrows on this map show the routes taken by explorers and pioneers between 1540 and 1806.

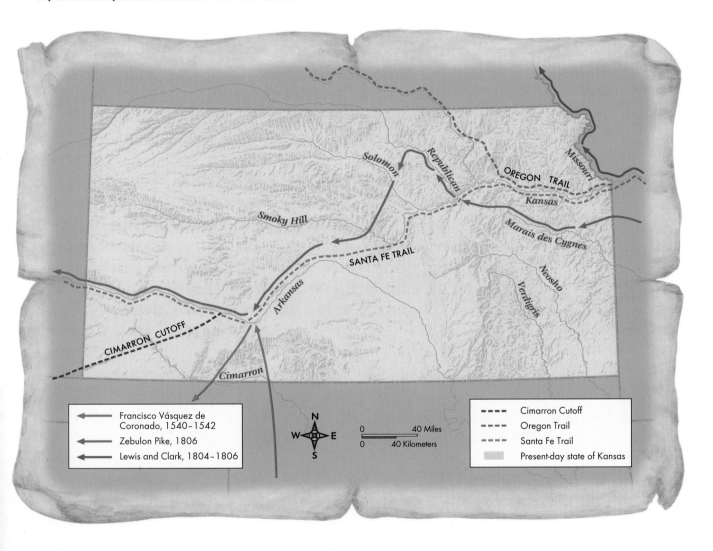

Francisco Vásquez de Coronado, 1540–1542

Zebulon Pike, 1806

Lewis and Clark, 1804–1806

Cimarron Cutoff

Oregon Trail

Santa Fe Trail

Present-day state of Kansas

ably did not visit Kansas, Jolliet and Marquette drew maps that showed parts of the area. Marquette's map included the names of the Kansa, Osage, Pawnee, and other Native American nations.

In 1682, the French explorer René-Robert Cavelier, Sieur de La Salle, claimed the lands west of the Mississippi River for France. He named the region Louisiana, in honor of France's king, Louis XIV. Louisiana included the region that is now Kansas.

The governor of Louisiana sent French explorer Charles Claude du Tisne to explore the Missouri River in 1719. Du Tisne visited Osage villages near the mouth of the Osage River. He also crossed the northeast corner of Kansas to Pawnee villages on the Republican River.

HORSES ON THE PLAINS

The Spanish rulers in New Mexico treated the Pueblo peoples like slaves. Enslaved American Indians learned how to take care of horses and how to ride them. In 1680, Pueblos in New Mexico revolted against the Spanish. When the Spanish fled the region, they left behind some of their horses. Soon, Zunis, one of the Pueblo peoples, were rais-

René-Robert Cavelier, Sieur de La Salle, claiming the Louisiana region for France

Native Americans used horses to transport supplies on a type of sled called a travois.

ing large herds of horses. They taught members of other Native American groups how to ride.

The Native Americans of the Plains now had a better way to travel. Before Coronado and his men arrived on horseback, the Plains Indians had never seen horses. They had always traveled on foot. They either carried their supplies, tied them to the backs of large dogs, or loaded them on a sled called a travois. A horse pulling a travois could carry many more supplies than a dog. It could also travel farther in a given period of time.

Horses helped Native Americans become better hunters, too. A man on horseback could hunt by himself. He didn't need others to help him.

This painting by Seth Eastman depicts a
bison hunter on horseback.

The Indians quickly understood the value of horses.
Some people called them "sacred dogs." Others called
them "elk dogs" because of the animals' great size. Indians
later traded horses as if they were money.

With horses, Native Americans could travel longer dis-
tances. Over time, Comanches, Kiowas, Cheyennes, and
Arapahos rode into western Kansas. Most arrived from the
north, searching for new hunting grounds after the U.S.
government forced them out of their territories. These
Natives all competed for land—and for horses.

SHIFTING POWER

By 1694, many French Canadian traders had traveled to
Kansas. The French traded tools, guns, and other goods
to the Native people in exchange for valuable animal
skins and furs. In 1744, France's Fort de Cavagnial
became the first European settlement in what is now
Kansas. Located along the Missouri River near present-
day Leavenworth, it was an important trading center.

The fort was also useful for military reasons. France, Spain, and Great Britain were locked in a struggle for control of North America. The fort's location allowed the French to keep Spain's traders and soldiers from traveling on the Missouri River.

In 1754, France and Great Britain went to war over control of trade in North America. This conflict was called the French and Indian War because many Native Americans fought with France against Great Britain. By 1762, the French were losing badly. To prevent the British from taking over the region, France **ceded** all of its land west of the Mississippi—including present-day Kansas—to Spain. Spain did not keep the region for long. In 1800, the land returned to French control. Then, just three years later, the United States purchased the Louisiana region from France. Kansas was now part of a new nation.

WORD TO KNOW

ceded *gave up or granted*

European traders camping with Native Americans and bartering for bison fur

READ ABOUT

Settlers traveled to
Kansas in covered
wagons and on
horseback.

1804 ▶

*American
explorers Lewis
and Clark, guided
by Sacagawea, pass
through Kansas*

1821

*William Becknell
opens the Santa
Fe Trail*

1854

*The Kansas-Nebraska
Act allows Kansas
residents to decide
about slavery*

GROWTH AND CHANGE

CHAPTER FOUR

GROWTH AND CHANGE

★

P EOPLE TRAVELED TO WHAT IS NOW KANSAS FOR A NUMBER OF REASONS. Native Americans were forced to relocate there from the East in the 1830s. When the land was opened to white settlers in 1854, they poured into the region to start new lives. Many African Americans arrived after the Civil War (1861–1865) to do the same.

1861 ►

Kansas becomes the 34th state

1879

Thousands of African Americans called exodusters migrate to Kansas

1912

Women in Kansas gain the right to vote in all elections

Louisiana Purchase

This map shows the area (in yellow) that made up the Louisiana Purchase and the present-day state of Kansas (in orange).

United States, 1803

Louisiana Purchase

United States Territory, 1803

Present-day state of Kansas

WORD TO KNOW

corps *a group working together on a special mission*

The Louisiana Purchase doubled the size of the United States.

AMERICAN EXPLORERS

In 1803, the United States bought Louisiana from France. President Thomas Jefferson wanted to know more about the vast territory he had just purchased. He asked his secretary, Captain Meriwether Lewis, to explore Louisiana and the land farther west. Lewis invited his friend Lieutenant William Clark to join him.

On May 14, 1804, Lewis and Clark's **Corps** of Discovery—which included more than 40 people—set out from St. Louis, Missouri, in boats. When the group landed near Kansa villages at the mouth of the Kansas River on June 26, they became the first European Americans to explore the region. On July 4, Lewis and Clark arrived at a stream near what is now the town of Atchison. They named the stream Independence Creek in honor of Independence Day and celebrated the holiday along its banks. The Corps of Discovery eventually explored all the way to the Pacific Ocean.

In 1806, Zebulon M. Pike, an officer in the U.S. Army, set out from St. Louis on another mission—to make peace with the Indians. He met with Osages in what is now western Missouri and with Pawnees on the Republican River. When he found a Spanish flag flying in one village, he

Explorers William Clark (left) and Meriwether Lewis with their guide, Sacagawea

replaced it with the American flag. In his journals, Pike compared the dry and windy High Plains to the "sandy deserts of Africa." A few years later, Major Stephen H. Long entered the region with scientists to record its plant and animal life. On his map, Long labeled the treeless prairie the "Great American Desert." People in other

A delegation of Kansa people discussing land issues with the commissioner of Indian affairs in Washington, D.C., 1857

WOW

In 1827, the U.S. government sent Daniel Morgan Boone—son of explorer Daniel Boone—to teach the Kansa people new farming methods. His son Napoleon was the first white child born in Kansas.

WORD TO KNOW

treaties *written agreements between two or more groups*

parts of the country formed their idea of Kansas from the descriptions of these early explorers.

NATIVE AMERICAN NEWCOMERS

White Americans in the East were eager for land. To satisfy this demand, President Andrew Jackson signed the Indian Removal Act in 1830. This act forced eastern Native Americans to move west of the Mississippi, to what are now Kansas and Oklahoma. The law promised that the lands in Kansas would belong to these newcomers "forever." The government signed unfair **treaties** with the Kansa and Osage nations so that they would give up much of their land in eastern Kansas for the new arrivals.

In all, almost 30 Native American nations had to leave their traditional lands in the Ohio River valley and Great Lakes region and settle in Kansas. These included Shawnees,

Delawares, Ojibwes, Wyandots, Pottawatomies, Miamis, Kickapoos, Ottawas, Foxes, Sacs, and Iowas.

Many **missionaries** followed the Native Americans into Kansas. They established missions where Native Americans were taught to live, speak, and work like European Americans. Some American Indians who had already been exposed to European Americans adopted some of their habits. Many other Indians resisted giving up their traditional ways of life. Some missionaries forced Indian children to live in boarding schools, away from their families.

HIGHWAYS TO THE WEST

In 1821, Captain William Becknell led a wagon train loaded with trade goods from Missouri to Santa Fe, New Mexico. This route to the Southwest, which ran all the way across Kansas, became known as the Santa Fe Trail.

The U.S. government wanted white traders to be able to travel freely along the trail. In 1825, the government signed a treaty with the Osage nation to ensure the safety of travelers. The government also signed a similar treaty with the Kansa.

By the 1850s, the Santa Fe Trail was a busy trade route. Indians and white traders and soldiers sometimes clashed along the trail. Indians were angry that these whites had taken over their hunting grounds.

Another route west, the Oregon Trail, ran from Missouri to Oregon across the northeast corner of Kansas. Settlers packed their belongings into ox-drawn covered wagons called prairie schooners and headed out across the plains. A schooner is a type of boat, and to these newcomers, the plains looked like a sea of grass. During the 1849 California gold rush, more than 90,000 people traveled through Kansas seeking their fortunes in the West.

Kansas's first newspaper, the *Shawnee Sun*, was printed in 1835 at the Shawnee Indian Baptist Mission near today's Kansas City. The newspaper was written in the Shawnee language.

WORD TO KNOW

missionaries *people who try to convert others to a religion*

SEE IT HERE!

THE SANTA FE TRAIL

From 1821 to 1880, the Santa Fe Trail was the busiest highway in the United States. Much of the nearly 900-mile (1,448 km) trading route from Missouri to New Mexico ran through Kansas. Today, you can still see traces of the trail. Deep ruts cut by wagon wheels run along the trail near Dodge City. These ruts serve as a reminder of just how many wagons took this route west.

Covered wagons in the town of Manhattan, 1860

Hollenberg Station, near Hanover, Kansas, is the last Pony Express station in the country still standing in its original location.

By the 1850s, people also crossed Kansas in stage-coaches, which were heavy, covered carriages drawn by four horses. Stagecoaches were also called mud wagons because they traveled easily over muddy trails.

In 1860, the Pony Express began delivering mail from Missouri to California. A rider would leave St. Joseph, Missouri, carrying mail in his saddlebags. During the coming days, that mail was transferred between riders at 190 relay stations, including several in Kansas. Mail could travel from St. Joseph, Missouri, to Sacramento, California—more than 2,000 miles (3,200 km)—in only 10 days. By October 1861, telegraph lines replaced the Pony Express.

KANSAS TERRITORY

As travelers passed through Kansas and saw the rich farm-land, many wanted to settle in the region. By treaty, the land belonged to Native Americans, and white settlers were not allowed to move there—but many did anyway.

In 1854, the U.S. government decided to change the law. It created Kansas and Nebraska territories and permitted white settlers to move there. Thousands of settlers arrived in Kansas the first year alone. Although the government had promised Kansas to the Native American nations "forever," they now had to move again. Before long, the government had forced nearly all Native American nations out of Kansas.

Now that Kansas was a territory, it could become a state—and it had to answer an important question. Would it allow slavery or not? Enslaved Africans had first been transported to what is now the United States in 1619. As the cotton trade grew in the South, **plantation** owners bought more and more enslaved workers. Slavery became an institution in the South. Meanwhile, slavery was disappearing from the North.

The Missouri Compromise of 1820 had prohibited slavery in any new states north and west of Missouri. Proslavery members of Congress believed the Missouri Compromise threatened the growth of slavery and their influence on the government. If the number of Free States increased but the number of Slave States did not, the power of the Slave States would diminish. To prevent this from happening, Congress passed the Kansas-Nebraska Act in 1854. This law allowed each territory to decide whether its **constitution** would allow slavery. After statehood was approved by the U.S. Congress, these constitutions would govern Kansas and Nebraska.

Some people from the Slave State of Missouri moved to the Kansas Territory so they could vote to ensure Kansas would be a Slave State. An antislavery group called the New England Emigrant Aid Company countered this action by sending antislavery settlers to the territory. They founded the towns of Lawrence and Topeka.

WORDS TO KNOW

plantation *a large farm that grows mainly one crop*

constitution *a written document that contains all the governing principles of a state or country*

A flyer from 1855

Q8 WHAT WERE THE FIRST ENGLISH-LANGUAGE NEWS-PAPERS IN KANSAS?

A8 The *Kansas Weekly Herald* began in Leavenworth in 1854. It was a proslavery paper. The *Kansas Tribune*, which was against slavery, was founded in 1855 in Lawrence.

BLEEDING KANSAS

On March 30, 1855, election day in Kansas Territory, 5,000 heavily armed supporters of slavery rode into Kansas from Missouri. Although they did not live in Kansas, these men, called Border Ruffians, illegally voted in the election. In fact, around twice as many people voted in this election as there were registered voters. Border Ruffians also threatened voters and election officials. Because of the Border Ruffians' votes, proslavery forces won the election. This was only the beginning of the fight over slavery in Kansas.

In 1856, Border Ruffians burned down a hotel in

Border Ruffians from Missouri entering Kansas to vote for slavery in 1855

the Free State town of Lawrence. They also destroyed the offices of two antislavery newspapers. Outraged, a man named John Brown led a raid on a group of pro-slavery settlers some 40 miles (64 km) east of Lawrence and killed five men. This event is known as the Pottawatomie Massacre. Brown was much hated in the South, but he became a hero among Kansas Free Staters, the people who opposed slavery.

On August 30, Brown and a group of supporters tried to defend the town of Osawatomie against an attack by a much larger group of proslavery men. The attackers burned the town, and Brown's son, Frederick, was one of several people killed. The fight over slavery continued in Kansas for two years, giving it the nickname Bleeding Kansas. In all, more than 50 people died.

Meanwhile, hundreds of African American men, women, and children who were escaping slavery traveled through Kansas on the Underground Railroad. Many enslaved people traveled along this route of secret hiding places to escape to freedom. Topeka and Lawrence were stops along the way. Some Kansans, including John Brown, crossed into Missouri to help free enslaved people. They were called Jayhawkers.

THE WYANDOTTE CONSTITUTION

In 1859, delegates gathered at Wyandotte (now part of Kansas City) to write another constitution. The Kansas Territory had already written three—but Congress had rejected all of them.

The constitution drafted at Wyandotte outlawed slavery. It also established the present-day borders of Kansas. Topeka was suggested as the state capital. Voters in Kansas approved the Wyandotte Constitution, and Congress admitted Kansas as the 34th state on January 29, 1861.

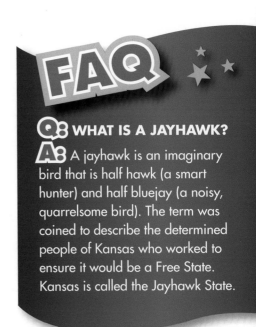

Q: WHAT IS A JAYHAWK?

A: A jayhawk is an imaginary bird that is half hawk (a smart hunter) and half bluejay (a noisy, quarrelsome bird). The term was coined to describe the determined people of Kansas who worked to ensure it would be a Free State. Kansas is called the Jayhawk State.

Kansas: From Territory to Statehood
(1854 to 1861)

This map shows the original Kansas Territory and the area that became the state of Kansas in 1861.

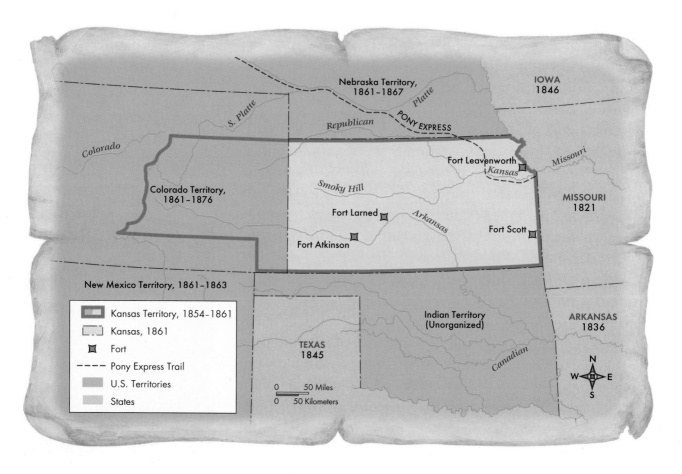

THE CIVIL WAR

Three months later, the American Civil War began partly over the issue of slavery—the very issue that had divided Kansas. The new Republican Party had formed to oppose the expansion of slavery into the West. Republican Abraham Lincoln of Illinois was elected president in 1860. Some Southerners feared he would end slavery. After he was elected, 11 Southern states withdrew from the Union and formed a new nation called the Confederate States of

America. In April 1861, Confederate troops fired on Fort Sumter in Charleston, South Carolina, starting the Civil War.

More than 20,000 Kansans served in the Civil War. Most of the war took place to the east, and Kansas soldiers fought in battles throughout the land, including at the Battle of Wilson's Creek in Missouri. Confederate **guerrillas** and bands of raiders called bushwhackers ambushed Kansas towns, including Humboldt, Gardner, and Olathe.

The Missouri-Kansas border was one of the bloodiest places during the war, as Jayhawkers confronted bushwhackers. In 1863, a proslavery raider named William C. Quantrill led 450 men—among them, the outlaw Frank James—on a raid on Lawrence, burning the town and killing more than 180 citizens. Quantrill's raid was one of the most brutal civilian massacres in the country during the Civil War.

NEW SETTLERS

The Civil War ended in April 1865. Slavery was now legally prohibited, but the end of the war did not mean

WORD TO KNOW

guerrillas *soldiers who don't belong to regular armies; they often use surprise attacks and other uncommon battle tactics*

Confederate guerrillas destroying the town of Lawrence in 1863

THE BATTLE OF MINE CREEK

The only military battle fought in Kansas was the Battle of Mine Creek, which occurred on October 25, 1864. Union soldiers were outnumbered almost three to one, but in 30 minutes they captured more than 600 Confederate soldiers. This was one of the largest **cavalry** battles of the Civil War.

WORD TO KNOW

cavalry *soldiers who ride on horseback*

the end of difficulties for African Americans in the South. By the late 1870s, Southern governments had begun passing laws to prevent African Americans from buying land. Plantation owners charged them high rents to lease farmland. African Americans also faced hostility and violence from hate groups such as the Ku Klux Klan and others.

As a result, many African Americans left the South. In the Exodus of 1879, African American families took part in a massive migration to Kansas. They hoped to build homes, buy land, educate their children, and live in peace in the state where the fight over slavery had been so brutal. About a year later, more than 40,000 African Americans had moved to Kansas to begin new lives.

These settlers were known as exodusters. Some of them settled in the capital of Topeka, while others founded new, all-black towns. African Americans from Kentucky founded the all-black town of Nicodemus in northwestern Kansas. In 1882, Nicodemus resident Edwin P. McCabe was elected state auditor, making him one of the highest-ranking elected African American officials in the 19th century.

Former slave families migrating to Kansas

The war's end also brought families from the eastern United States and from England, Germany, Norway, Sweden, and Russia. The Homestead Act of 1862 encouraged settlers to travel west. It promised them 160 acres (65 ha) of land if they paid a small fee, lived on the land for five years, farmed it, and built a house on it.

In 1869, Swedish farmers settled in Smoky Valley. They founded the town of Lindsborg, which today is also known as Little Sweden. German-Russian immigrants who followed the Mennonite faith brought a type of hardy winter wheat called turkey red. Turkey red grew well on the plains and soon became the region's most important wheat variety. Kansas became one of the nation's top wheat-growing states.

MINI-BIO

BENJAMIN "PAP" SINGLETON: LEADER OF THE EXODUSTERS

Benjamin Singleton (1809–1892) was born into slavery in Tennessee. He escaped in 1846 and helped other African Americans make their way to freedom in Canada. After the Civil War, Singleton traveled throughout the South, spreading the word about Kansas. He formed two colonies there for African Americans. By 1880, he had brought 7,432 people to Kansas.

? **Want to know more?** Visit www.factsfor now.scholastic.com and enter the keyword **Kansas**.

ECONOMIC GROWTH

By 1870, the population of Kansas had soared to 365,000. The state was booming. Several colleges had been founded. Coal mines were operating in the state. There were woolen mills at Lawrence and Fort Scott and a cotton gin at Burlington. By this time, several railroad companies had laid tracks in the state.

Cyrus K. Holliday had started the Atchison and Topeka Railroad Company in 1859. By 1872, it was called the Atchison, Topeka, and Santa Fe Railroad and ran all the way across Kansas. It grew to become one of the largest railroad lines in the country. Another railroad, the Kansas Pacific, became part of the Union Pacific Railroad, which ran from Lawrence to Denver, Colorado.

Between 1860 and 1890, the population of Kansas grew from about 100,000 to more than 1.4 million.

Trains brought many more settlers to Kansas. They also carried cattle. In 1867, a cattle buyer named Joseph G. McCoy set up a stockyard in Abilene, along the Union Pacific Railroad. Within a year, he had shipped 35,000 head of cattle east.

For the next 20 years, Kansas was cow country. Cowboys drove cattle from Texas into Kansas along the Chisholm and Western trails. The cattle were shipped east from towns such as Abilene and Dodge City. The rowdy lifestyle of the cowboys in these cattle shipping towns, known as cowtowns, created the legendary Wild West.

At the end of the long cattle drive, cowboys spent their free time in dance halls, gambling parlors, and saloons. Many outlaws were also drawn to these towns. Fights were common, and lawmen worked hard to keep order. Bat Masterson, Wyatt Earp, and Wild Bill Hickok all worked as marshals in Kansas cowtowns.

NEW DIRECTIONS

In 1886, Kansas was hit by a series of blizzards. Eighty percent of the state's cattle froze to death, speeding the end of the

WOW

In 1874, the skies of Kansas were black with grasshoppers for several days. The insect infestation caused major damage to the region's crops.

MINI-BIO

WILD BILL HICKOK: LAWMAN

James Butler "Wild Bill" Hickok (1837–1876) was born in Illinois. He fought slavery with the Free Staters of Kansas and served in the Civil War with Kansas soldiers in the Battle of Wilson's Creek. In 1871, he became marshal of Abilene. Wild Bill wasn't afraid to confront trouble-makers. His bravery and kindness made him a town hero—and a legend of the Wild West.

 Want to know more? Visit www.factsfornow .scholastic.com and enter the keyword **Kansas**.

BUFFALO BILL'S WILD WEST SHOW

Kansan William F. "Buffalo Bill" Cody earned his nickname from supplying the U.S. Army and railroad workers with bison meat. He was also a trapper, Civil War soldier, and Pony Express rider. Buffalo Bill later founded a traveling Wild West show, which featured cowboys, cowgirls (including Annie Oakley), and Native American leaders such as Geronimo and Sitting Bill.

Wyatt Earp (front, second from left) was part of a group of peacekeepers in Dodge City in the late 1800s.

great cattle era. Soon afterward, a severe drought struck Kansas, causing crops to fail.

Kansas recovered quickly. In 1889, the state produced the largest corn crop in its history. It also began to produce beet sugar and salt. Kansas apples, grown in orchards in the eastern part of the state, won awards. Meanwhile, industry grew. Kansas workers made bricks and brought oil up from the ground.

The state was growing in other ways, too. Kansas was one of the first states in the country to give women the right to vote in some elections. In 1861, Kansas women could vote in local school elections, and by 1887, they could vote in city elections and run for office. That year, Susanna Madora Salter of Argonia became the first woman mayor in the United States. In 1912, Kansas became the eighth state to grant complete **suffrage** to women—eight years before women's right to vote became law across the United States.

WORD TO KNOW

suffrage *the right to vote*

WORD TO KNOW

foreclosures *legal processes for taking back property when the payment for it is overdue*

POPULISTS AND PROGRESSIVES

In the late 19th century, farmers in Kansas and throughout the country earned less for their corn, wheat, and cotton, but had to pay more for equipment and shipping on the railroads. Each year brought greater debt and hardship. From 1889 to 1893, Kansas suffered 11,123 **foreclosures**. In two years, banks took back 90 percent of the farmland in 15 of the state's more than 100 counties.

The farmers claimed that railroad owners and bankers were becoming wealthy at their expense. They believed that the rich had taken control of the government. To protect their rights, they formed an organization called the Granger movement, and later one called the Farmers' Alliance. The Grangers pressured state legislators to protect farmers' interests. Farmers' Alliance members eventually formed a national political party called the People's Party, or Populist Party, to stand up for working men and women. In 1892 and 1896, Populists joined with Democrats to elect the state's governors.

In the early part of the 20th century, the progressive movement continued the fight for social and political reforms, in Kansas and across the nation. Progressives wanted to protect all types of laborers and stop political corruption. The movement helped establish child labor laws.

MINI-BIO

MARY ELIZABETH LEASE: POPULIST LEADER

"Raise less corn and more hell!" Mary Elizabeth Lease (1850–1933) was famous for lines like this in her speeches to Kansas farmers. She urged them to fight for their rights and protest the high railroad and loan rates that threatened their survival. She believed that the farmers should form alliances to increase their power against wealthy corporations. Lease, who had been a teacher before she became a leader in the Populist movement, also wanted women to have the right to vote. Her strong opinions earned her the nickname Mary Yellin' Lease.

 Want to know more? Visit www.factsfornow .scholastic.com and enter the keyword **Kansas**.

In Kansas City, a crowd waves to soldiers heading out to join American forces in World War I.

Meanwhile, some citizens, most notably Carry Nation, led the cause of temperance, the prohibition of alcohol.

THE WAR EFFORT

During World War I (1914–1918), tens of thousands of Kansans served in the U.S. military. U.S. soldiers trained at Fort Leavenworth and Camp Funston at Fort Riley. Kansas provided the government with helium, a gas that is lighter than air, which was used to fly military aircraft called dirigibles, or blimps. The U.S. government declared, "Food will win the war!" and Kansas provided it. Kansas wheat and beef fed American soldiers and people in Europe, where the war was being fought. When World War I ended in 1918, a new era began in the United States—and in Kansas, too.

READ ABOUT

Severe dust storms
swept across Kansas
during the 1930s.

1920s ▲
*Kansas's aircraft
industry flourishes*

1930s
*Severe drought
produces huge
dust storms
across Kansas*

1951
*Flooding
damages or
destroys 45,000
homes in
Kansas*

1954
*The U.S. Supreme
Court rules that
school segregation
is illegal in
Brown v. Board
of Education of
Topeka*

CHAPTER FIVE

MORE MODERN TIMES

★

T HE TRANSLATION OF THE KANSAS MOTTO IS "TO THE STARS THROUGH DIFFICULTIES!" Early Kansans had faced difficult times—Native Americans were forced off their land, violent arguments raged over slavery, and blizzards wiped out the cattle industry. In the 20th century, although Kansas continued to struggle, it headed "to the stars" as agriculture boomed, industry flourished, and Kansans made plans for the future.

1956
The Kansas Turnpike opens

1970 ▶
Nearly two-thirds of Kansans live in cities

2014
Former governor Kathleen Sebelius resigns as U.S. secretary of health and human services

FAQ ★ ★ ★

Q8 WHAT IS A BARNSTORMER?

A8 A barnstormer is a pilot who performs airplane stunts. Barnstorming was popular in the 1920s. Stunt pilots would fly upside down, make giant loops, and perform other tricks as people watched from the ground. Sometimes several planes performed together as a "flying circus."

THE ROARING TWENTIES

After World War I ended in 1918, the country prospered. In fact, the 1920s were known as the Roaring Twenties. It was a time of new inventions and new activities. People listened to radios in their homes and began to go to movie theaters. A new American music form called jazz drew audiences to dance halls and clubs.

During the Roaring Twenties, Kansas roared, too—with the sounds of engines in the sky. Jake Moellendick, a barnstormer named E. M. Laird, and their partner, William Burke, started an airplane company in Wichita. Laird designed a new plane that could carry a pilot and two passengers. First flown in 1920, the Laird Swallow was the first commercial airplane in the country and marked the beginning of Wichita's aircraft industry.

MINI-BIO

AMELIA EARHART: PIONEERING PILOT

Amelia Earhart (1897–1937) was born in Atchison. She took her first ride in an airplane in 1920. She was determined to learn to fly and began taking lessons the following year. In 1932, she became the first woman to fly alone across the Atlantic Ocean. In 1937, she set out to fly around the world. She was about three-quarters of the way through the trip when her plane disappeared over the Pacific Ocean. It has never been found.

? Want to know more? Visit www.factsfornow.scholastic.com and enter the keyword **Kansas**.

Airplane manufacturer Clyde Cessna works on an aircraft in 1927.

An automobile parade at the Pratt County Fair in 1909

As some Kansans flew through the skies, others sped along on land. In 1903, the Ford Motor Company produced its first car. By the 1920s, automobiles were widespread in Kansas and many other parts of the country. In 1925, Walter P. Chrysler, who was born in Wamego, started the Chrysler Corporation. By 1935, it was the second-largest auto manufacturer in the world.

Along with the rest of the country, Kansas soon needed better roads. By the end of 1925, the federal and state governments had built roads across the state. Some were built with fine pieces of chert or flint mined in the state's southeastern corner. By 1928, more than 124,000 miles (200,000 km) of roads crossed Kansas.

DARK DAYS

Despite the activity and growth during the 1920s, the country's economy was weak. In 1929, a growing economic crisis called the Great Depression turned into

If all the public roads and highways in Kansas were stretched out in one straight line, they would reach more than halfway to the moon!

A dust storm roaring through a Kansas town in 1935

worldwide panic when the U.S. stock market crashed. Banks failed, and the people who had put their money in the banks lost all their savings. Factories shut down. Many companies, including several of the aircraft companies in Kansas, went out of business. Over the course of the Depression, which lasted through the 1930s, more than 15 million Americans lost their jobs. In cities from New York to San Francisco, people stood in lines to get free bread and soup for themselves and their families. The Depression also hurt the nation's farms. Crop prices dropped. Then, to make matters worse for Kansas farmers, it stopped raining.

The drought began in 1931. Crops withered as temperatures soared and no rain fell. Western Kansas became as dry as a desert. During World War I, farmers in Kansas had plowed thousands of acres of grassland to grow more wheat. Without the prairie grass to hold the soil in place, the fierce Kansas wind picked it up and carried it away.

In 1934—the worst year of the drought—devastating dust storms began. Winds of 40 to 50 miles (64 to 80 km) per hour produced "black blizzards," which darkened the skies of western Kansas. There was so much dirt in the air that people standing in their backyards couldn't find their houses. Some even suffocated from inhaling the fine dust.

The droughts and dust storms lasted for nine years, a period called the Dust Bowl. The states that were hardest hit included Kansas, Oklahoma, Texas, New Mexico, and Colorado. More than 3 million people left the Great Plains during the Dust Bowl, but Kansans had been through hard times before, and many stayed to rebuild their lives.

The drought and the dust storms finally ended in 1939. Kansas farmers began planting crops that would hold the soil in place during high winds. They learned new ways to farm and to conserve water, so any future droughts and storms would be less destructive. The federal and state governments worked together to revive the buffalo grass pastures of western Kansas.

During the dust storms of the 1930s, soil from Kansas blew all the way across the country to the Atlantic Ocean.

A Wilburton farmer with his tractor, which is buried in sand following droughts and dust storms

ANOTHER WAR

World War II began in Europe and Asia in 1939. At first, the United States stayed out of the war. Then, in 1941, Japan bombed the U.S. Navy base at Pearl Harbor, Hawai'i, and the United States declared war. The United States and its **allies** needed weapons and ammunition. Soldiers needed airplanes, tanks, and uniforms. All across the country, factories were churning out goods to support the war effort. This increased activity pulled the country out of the Great Depression.

The government built new military sites in Kansas. Soldiers trained at Fort Riley and Fort Leavenworth. Navy pilots trained on bases in Olathe and Hutchinson. Kansas farmers once again shipped millions of tons of wheat to feed soldiers and civilians in Europe. The state's aircraft companies produced thousands of military aircraft, employing more than 25,000 workers. Many men were at war, so the majority of the workers were women. Across the United States, 6 million women worked in factories during the war.

During World War II, men and women worked in factories, such as this Boeing Airplane Company plant in Wichita.

More than 215,000 Kansans served in the military during World War II. One of them, General Dwight D. Eisenhower, served as the supreme commander of the Allied forces in Europe. After the war ended, Eisenhower visited his home state and said, "The proudest thing I can say today is that I'm from Abilene." In 1952, he was elected president of the United States.

ALL EYES ON KANSAS

After the Civil War, Southern states had passed several **segregation** laws that separated institutions by race. Segregation was common throughout the rest of the country, too. Under these laws, black and white Americans had to attend different schools. In Kansas, the law did not insist on segregation, but cities with populations of more than 15,000 could establish separate elementary schools for black and white children—and Topeka did just that.

In 1951, the Reverend Oliver Brown and 13 other parents sued the Topeka Board of Education. Brown's seven-year-old daughter, Linda, was not allowed to attend a nearby all-white school. Instead, she had to walk past dangerous train tracks just to get to the bus that would take her several miles to a school for African American children. The case, called *Brown v. Board of Education of Topeka*, went before the U.S. Supreme Court. In 1954, the Court ruled that separate schools for black and white students violated the Fourteenth **Amendment** to the U.S. Constitution. This amendment

MINI-BIO

WILLIAM ALLEN WHITE: JOURNALIST AND POLITICIAN

William Allen White (1868–1944) was born in Emporia. After attending the University of Kansas, he began writing **editorials** for a newspaper in Kansas City. In 1895, he bought the Emporia Gazette, where he continued to write editorials. He ran for governor in 1924. He wanted to do something about the Ku Klux Klan, calling it a "menace to peace . . . [and] decent neighborly living." White lost the election, but he focused the country's attention on the issue of racism. In 1923, he won the Pulitzer Prize for his writing.

 Want to know more? Visit www.factsfornow .scholastic.com and enter the keyword **Kansas**.

WORDS TO KNOW

segregation *separation from others according to race, class, ethnic group, religion, or other factors*

editorials *newspaper articles that give the opinion of a paper's editor or publisher*

amendment *a change to a law or legal document*

Linda Brown (foreground), shown at the Monroe Elementary School, was not allowed to attend an all-white school until her father and other parents sued the Topeka school board.

states that laws must protect all people equally. The Court ruled that by segregating black and white schoolchildren, the state was not protecting the right of African American children to have the same education as white children.

The ruling made school segregation illegal across the country. The Court's decision was a key event in the civil rights movement, the struggle to ensure equal rights for all Americans, regardless of race.

LOOKING AHEAD

After World War II ended in 1945, Kansas's industries continued to boom. The aircraft industry created new jobs, and Kansas companies began to produce planes that would carry passengers and cargo. Newly constructed highways made it easier for people to travel.

In 1951, record rainfall produced flooding in the Kansas River basin. In Kansas and Missouri, the floods caused billions of dollars in damage. Around 45,000 Kansan homes were damaged or destroyed. Engineers built dams on several Kansas rivers to protect the state from future floods.

In the 1960s and 1970s, Kansas farms produced more crops than ever. Farmers had new and better technology, so they needed fewer workers. By 1970, almost two-thirds of the people in Kansas lived in urban areas. During this time, small family farms throughout the nation faced serious challenges. Many farmers were in debt to banks from which they had borrowed money. Farmers who could not repay their loans lost their farms. Energy costs were high, and there was an ongoing drought that hurt crop production.

Farmers formed the American Agriculture Movement (AAM), which worked to alert politicians and the public

A view of modern Wichita

that earning a living on the family farm was nearly impossible. In January 1978, 3,000 farmers from Kansas and elsewhere drove their tractors to Washington, D.C., to make their point. Another "tractorcade" protest in Washington took place the following year. By the 1980s, the federal government instituted programs to assist American farmers, but to this day, many small Kansas family farms find it difficult to survive.

Kansas has changed in other ways as well. Hispanics have been the fastest-growing ethnic group in the state. Between 2000 and 2010, the Hispanic population in Kansas grew by 59 percent. Many Hispanic people arrived from Mexico and from elsewhere in the United States to work in meatpacking plants in western Kansas.

Kansas continues to rely on the spirit of its people. As former governor Kathleen Sebelius, who served as U.S. secretary of health and human services until 2014, said, "Kansas's destiny . . . won't be determined by its factories or farms, offices or assembly lines. No, our state's destiny lies with its people—with all of us."

READ ABOUT

Enjoying a water
ride at the Kansas
State Fair

CHAPTER SIX

PEOPLE

★

AS DOROTHY SAYS IN *THE WIZARD OF OZ*, "THERE'S NO PLACE LIKE HOME"—ESPECIALLY WHEN HOME IS KANSAS! Part of what makes Kansas so special is the diverse mix of people who live there. Some moved to Kansas from other states. Others came from as far away as Sweden, Mexico, and the Pacific Islands. In the state's festivals, art, and fast-moving games, the rich culture and spirit of Kansas shines through.

Big City Life

This list shows the population of Kansas's biggest cities.

Wichita	382,368
Overland Park	173,372
Kansas City	145,786
Topeka	127,473
Olathe	125,872

Source: U.S. Census Bureau, 2010 census

CITY LIFE

In the 30 years after Kansas became a state, its population doubled nearly 14 times. Kansas has been growing steadily ever since. Although much of Kansas is farmland, 74 percent of Kansans live in cities. All of Kansas's large cities are in the eastern half of the state. As of 2012, 28 of the state's 105 counties had fewer than 3,500 people. Twenty-two of those counties are in the west.

Youngsters play in the Steckline-Lair Fountain at the Kansas State Fair in Hutchinson.

Kansans from many backgrounds take part in Oktoberfest celebrations.

A RICH HERITAGE

Nearly 40 percent of Kansans are of German ancestry. Many still live in towns that have the German names early settlers gave them: Stuttgart, Humboldt, Bern, and Bremen, to name a few. One of the largest celebrations of German culture is Oktoberfest, a festival held each fall on the state fairgrounds in Hays, the German capital of Kansas. Visitors come to hear German folk music, admire traditional crafts such as wooden cuckoo clocks, and eat sausages and other German foods.

The most recent German-speaking immigrants are Mennonites from Mexico. The Mennonites are a Protestant group that formed in central Europe in the 1500s. Since the early 1990s, Mennonite families have moved from Chihuahua, Mexico, to Sublette and other parts of southwestern Kansas. Many of them speak a form of German called *Plautdietsch*, or Low German, which is hundreds of years old. This old language is now spoken more in Kansas than in Germany.

TWIN CITIES

Kansas City is a twin city. Kansas City, Missouri, sits right across the Missouri River from Kansas City, Kansas. The two cities are almost like one large city. They share restaurants, cultural events, sports teams, and a bus system.

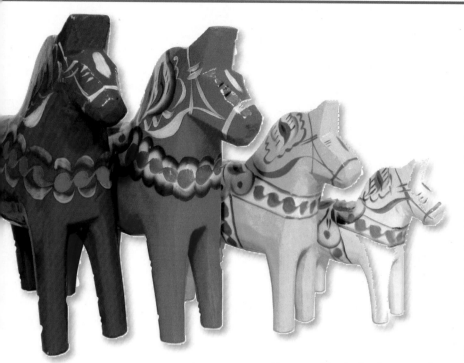

Dala horses

Many people in Strawberry Hill, a section of Kansas City, are descendants of immigrants from Croatia, a country in southern Europe. Marijana Grisnik is an artist whose grandparents are from Croatia. Grisnik paints scenes from her memories of growing up in Strawberry Hill. The community is also home to people from Lithuania, Poland, Slovakia, Slovenia, Russia, and the Netherlands.

When Swedish immigrants first arrived in Kansas, they called their new home *framtidslandet*, which means "the land of the future." Today, the town of Lindsborg in central Kansas is known as Little Sweden. Large, red painted wooden Dala horses, the symbol of Sweden, decorate the downtown streets. Every June, the town holds a Midsummer's Day Festival with traditional Swedish food, dance, and music.

More than 10 percent of Kansans are Hispanic, the fastest-growing ethnic group in Kansas. Most Hispanics in Kansas trace their origins to Mexico. Kansas City celebrates the Mexican holiday Cinco de Mayo with one of the largest Hispanic festivals in the Midwest. Every year since 1933, Topeka has had a Fiesta Mexicana, a five-day festival with dance, music, and traditional foods such as tacos and tamales. Emporia, Garden City, and Wichita also have large Mexican American populations.

Large numbers of African Americans first came to Kansas in the 1870s. Almost all of the all-black communities they founded have since disappeared. Only the town

Where Kansans Live

The colors on this map indicate population density throughout the state.
The darker the color, the more people live there.

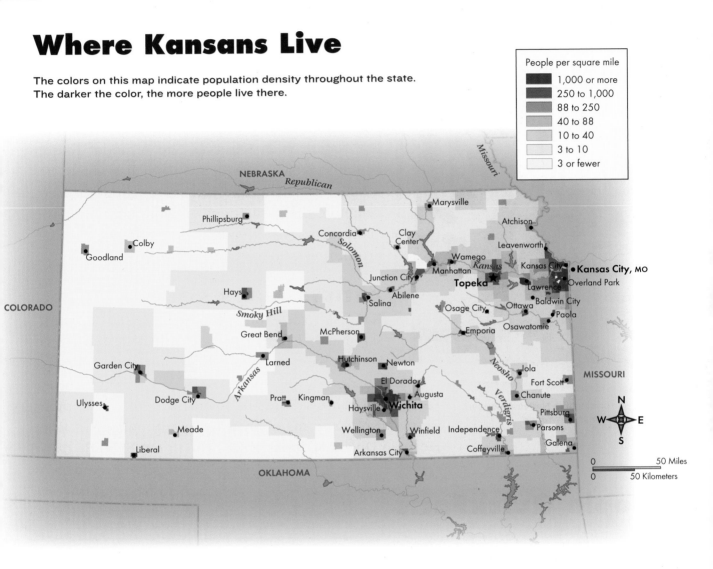

People per square mile
- 1,000 or more
- 250 to 1,000
- 88 to 250
- 40 to 88
- 10 to 40
- 3 to 10
- 3 or fewer

of Nicodemus remains, with fewer than 40 residents. Today, there are large African American communities in Kansas City, Wichita, Topeka, and smaller cities around the state. African Americans make up almost 6 percent of the state's total population.

More than 2 percent of Kansans are of Asian descent. Most come from the Philippines, Vietnam, China, India, Cambodia, Laos, and Thailand.

A student performing in a Native American dance competition in Lawrence

Native Americans make up less than 1 percent of Kansas's population. The Kickapoo Nation is based in Horton, the Iowa Tribe of Kansas and Nebraska is in White Cloud, the Prairie Band Potawatomi Nation is in Mayetta, and the Sac and Fox Nation is in Reserve. The Wyandot Nation of Kansas, based in Kansas City, has about 400 members. Native Americans throughout the state celebrate their traditions with annual powwows, gatherings that feature storytelling, singing, drumming, and dancing.

ARTISTS AND WRITERS

Kansas artists express their creativity with paint, scrap metal, concrete, and even Kansas crops! Some, like well-known painter John Steuart Curry, studied painting for years. Many other Kansas artists are self-taught. Robert Dorris built 15 dinosaurs out of scrap metal on his property outside of Erie. Herman Divers of Topeka built a chair out of bottle caps, and a motorcycle and two-seat car from aluminum-can pull tabs. Stanley J. Herd, from Protection, is an environmental artist. He makes "earthworks" by planting or mowing designs into fields. His work can be seen only when flying overhead. To celebrate Amelia Earhart's 100th birthday in 1997, he made a portrait of Earhart using plants, stone, and other natural materials.

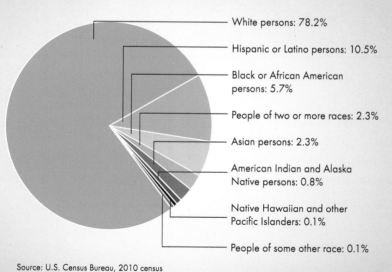

People QuickFacts

White persons: 78.2%

Hispanic or Latino persons: 10.5%

Black or African American persons: 5.7%

People of two or more races: 2.3%

Asian persons: 2.3%

American Indian and Alaska Native persons: 0.8%

Native Hawaiian and other Pacific Islanders: 0.1%

People of some other race: 0.1%

Source: U.S. Census Bureau, 2010 census

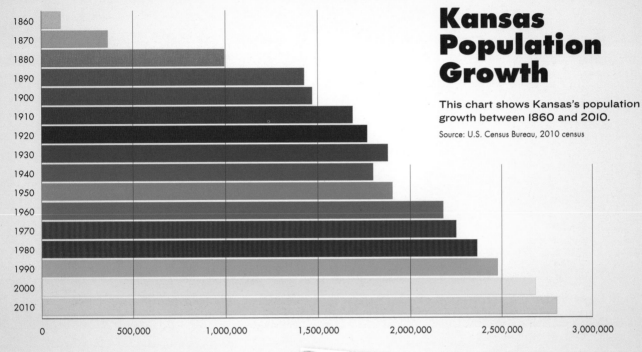

Kansas Population Growth

This chart shows Kansas's population growth between 1860 and 2010.

Source: U.S. Census Bureau, 2010 census

Writer William Edgar Stafford, born in Hutchinson, sometimes camped by the Cimarron River when he was in high school. He never forgot how it felt to be in the wide-open spaces of Kansas. He later wrote many poems about Kansas life and landscapes, including "Coronado Heights," "Prairie Town," and "Across Kansas." Stafford won the National Book Award in 1963.

Gwendolyn Brooks was another prize-winning Kansas poet. In 1950, she won the Pulitzer Prize for her book

MINI-BIO

JOHN STEUART CURRY: PAINTER

John Steuart Curry (1897–1946) was born on a farm near Dunavant. He began painting as a young boy and later studied at the Kansas City Art Institute and in New York, Chicago, and Paris. Curry is known for his scenes of tornadoes, floods, and everyday Kansas life. A 1929 flood near Lawrence inspired a series of paintings called Sanctuary. He also painted murals of Kansas history in the statehouse in Topeka, including one of antislavery leader John Brown and the days of Bleeding Kansas (shown here).

? **Want to know more?** Visit www.factsfornow .scholastic.com and enter the keyword **Kansas**.

Prize-winning poet Gwendolyn Brooks at her typewriter

MINI-BIO

GORDON PARKS: FILMMAKER

At age 25, Gordon Parks (1912–2006) taught himself how to use a camera. He became the first African American photographer featured in *Life* magazine. In 1969, he directed *The Learning Tree*, a film based on his book about a boy growing up in Kansas. Parks, who was born in Fort Scott, was awarded the National Medal of Arts in 1988.

? Want to know more? Visit www.factsfornow.scholastic.com and enter the keyword **Kansas**.

Annie Allen, a series of poems about an African American girl. Brooks was the first African American to win a Pulitzer Prize.

Poet and novelist Langston Hughes was born in Missouri but grew up in Lawrence and Topeka. His novel *Not Without Laughter* is about a young African American boy in a small Kansas town.

Several children's writers have set their works in Kansas. Cynthia Leitich Smith was born in Kansas City, Missouri, and attended the University of Kansas. Her novel *Rain Is Not My Indian Name* is the story of a young photographer in a small Kansas town who learns about her Native American heritage. The author belongs to the Muscogee (Creek) Nation. She won the 2001 Writer of the Year award from Wordcraft Circle of Native Writers and

Storytellers. Richard W. Jennings, who lives in Overland Park, wrote *The Great Whale of Kansas*. The book tells the story of a boy in Melville who finds the remains of an ancient ocean creature while digging in his backyard.

LEARNING IN KANSAS

The Wyandot people built the first free school in Kansas (then Indian Territory) in 1844 in what is now the county of Wyandotte. This one-room log schoolhouse stood until 1852. Schools became more common in the state after 1855, when Kansas Territory organized school districts.

Kansas has come a long way since then. Today, the state has hundreds of public schools and six state universities. The University of Kansas, in Lawrence, is the largest. Kansas State University in Manhattan was founded in 1863 as the state agricultural college. Today, its College of Agriculture is one

Writer Langston Hughes grew up in Lawrence and Topeka.

The campus at Haskell Indian Nations University in Lawrence

of the country's best. Haskell Indian Nations University was established in Lawrence in 1884 as an agricultural primary school for 22 Native American children. In 2013, the school had more than 1,000 students from many of the nation's Native American groups.

PLAYING IN KANSAS

Kansas is famous for all things basketball. The state has produced some of the greatest players and coaches. James Naismith, called the Father of Basketball, invented the game while working in Massachusetts in 1891. He formed the first men's basketball team in 1898 at the University of Kansas, where he coached for almost 40 years. Today, the University of Kansas Jayhawks are among the most successful college basketball teams in history. In 2008, the men's team captured the NCAA championship by defeating the University of Memphis.

Gale Sayers, the "Kansas Comet"

MINI-BIO

VICTOR ORTIZ: "VICIOUS" VICTOR

Introduced to boxing at age seven, "Vicious" Victor Ortiz (1987—) always knew he would be a world champion. He had a tough childhood growing up in Garden City, but he never stopped training. In April 2011, he beat the odds when he won over Andre Berto and became champion of the world in his weight class. The victory inspired the Kansas governor to name May 10 Victor Ortiz Day in the state. Ortiz has won 29 matches, 22 of them by knocking out his opponent, and lost five matches. In 2013, he demonstrated new skills competing on Dancing with the Stars.

? Want to know more? Visit www.factsfornow .scholastic.com and enter the keyword **Kansas**.

Kansas has also produced great baseball and football players. Walter "Big Train" Johnson, born in Humboldt, was one of the greatest pitchers of all time. He was one of the first players elected to the Baseball Hall of Fame. Football great Gale Sayers of Wichita earned the nickname Kansas Comet when he played for the University of Kansas. He later scored 22 touchdowns in his rookie year with the Chicago Bears and became the youngest player ever elected to the Football Hall of Fame. Lynette Woodard of Wichita is one of the greatest players in the history of women's basketball.

HOW TO TALK LIKE A KANSAN

Here are a few of the expressions you might hear in parts of Kansas.

The main street is sometimes called the "gut." Young people driving along main street for fun are "dragging the gut."

Big sandwiches made on long, thick rolls are called "subs," "hoagies," or "poor boys."

Centipedes are called "1,000-leg worms."

A long-legged spider is called a "grand-daddy longlegs."

Soft drinks are called "pop."

HOW TO EAT LIKE A KANSAN

In Kansas restaurants, you can find everything from chili and tacos to pizza and pie. Kansas produces a lot of wheat, and Kansans are proud of their breads. Every two years, the state hosts the Kansas Festival of Breads to celebrate its largest crop. Some of the winning recipes have been sunflower coffee cake, whole wheat honey loaf, and peanut butter cinnamon rolls. This flour-milling state is a big fan of cakes and cookies, too.

Stirring an entry at the Kansas State Fair Chili Cook-off

MENU

WHAT'S ON THE MENU IN KANSAS?

★ ★ ★

Barbecue

Kansas City loves barbecue. Before it's cooked, the meat is sometimes rubbed with spices. Then it's roasted for a long time over a hickory wood or charcoal fire and coated with a thick sweet-and-sour sauce.

Black Walnut Pie

Black walnut trees grow throughout eastern Kansas. It's not easy to remove the large shell—and the hulls will dye your fingers yellow—but the nut inside is delicious. Kansans eat the nuts plain or add them to candies, cookies, and even ice cream. Black walnut pie is a favorite.

Hot Apple Fritters

Apple fritters are apple slices that are coated with milk, flour, and spices and deep-fried until golden brown. Then they're dusted with powdered sugar. It's best to eat them while they're still hot!

Chicken-Fried Steak

Chicken or steak? This favorite is the best of both. A piece of steak is dipped into a milk batter and hand-coated with flour. The meat is then pan-fried until it is as crispy as fried chicken.

TRY THIS RECIPE
Caramel Corn

This crunchy treat is made with popcorn. Most of the world's popcorn is grown in Kansas and other nearby states.

Ingredients:
8 cups popped popcorn
1 cup butter
1 cup brown sugar, firmly packed
½ cup corn syrup
1 teaspoon baking soda

Instructions:
1. Preheat the oven to 250°F.
2. Pour the popcorn into a large roasting pan.
3. Put the butter, brown sugar, corn syrup, and baking soda in an extra-large saucepan. (The baking soda will cause the mixture to foam.)
4. Heat the mixture over medium heat, stirring constantly.
5. Remove the pan from the heat and allow the mixture to cool for 5 minutes.
6. Pour the caramel mixture over the popcorn and gently stir until mixed.
7. Bake the popcorn for 45 minutes, stirring every 15 minutes.
8. Remove the pan from the oven and pour the popcorn mixture onto waxed paper.
9. Allow the mixture to cool. Break it into pieces and eat.

Apple fritters

Caramel corn

READ ABOUT

The Senate Chamber inside the state capitol in Topeka.

CHAPTER SEVEN

GOVERNMENT

★

YOUNG PEOPLE IN KANSAS HAVE MANY WAYS TO LEARN ABOUT HOW THEIR STATE GOVERNMENT WORKS. Several programs—such as teen courts and mock trial contests—teach kids about the legal system and what happens in a courtroom. The program Kids Voting Kansas gives students a chance to "vote" in state and national elections. All Kansas citizens, no matter what their age, play an important role in shaping their state and nation.

THE CONSTITUTION

A constitution is a document that describes how a government will be organized. Kansans wrote four different constitutions during the early days of the Kansas Territory. The fourth, known as the Wyandotte Constitution, enabled Kansas to become a state.

The state's constitution has been changed more than 80 times. An amendment is made to a constitution

Capitol Facts

Here are some fascinating facts about Kansas's state capitol.

Exterior height: 306 feet (93 m)
Number of stories high: 5
Height of dome: 54.5 feet (17 m)
Number of steps to the dome: 296
Length: 386 feet (118 m)
Width: 399 feet (122 m)
Construction dates: 1866–1903
Cost of construction: $3.2 million

In the 21st century, the state capitol went through a series of renovations, including having its copper dome and roof replaced.

WOW The statue on the capitol dome depicts a Kansa warrior named Ad Astra. The name is taken from the state motto, *Ad astra per aspera*, "To the stars through difficulties." The statue faces the North Star.

Capital City

This map shows places of interest in Topeka, Kansas's capital city.

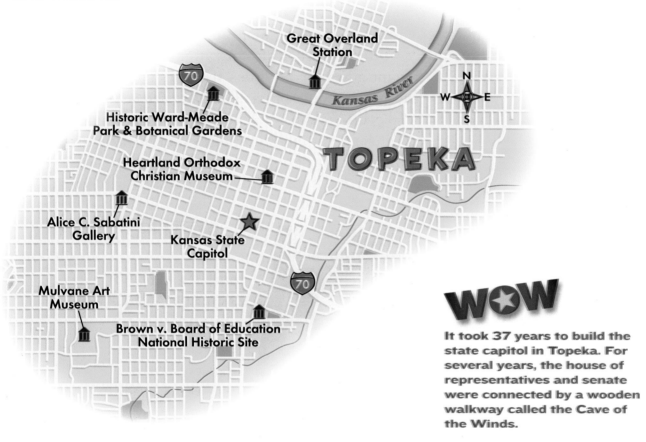

Great Overland Station

Historic Ward-Meade Park & Botanical Gardens

Heartland Orthodox Christian Museum

Alice C. Sabatini Gallery

Kansas State Capitol

Mulvane Art Museum

Brown v. Board of Education National Historic Site

Kansas River

TOPEKA

WOW

It took 37 years to build the state capitol in Topeka. For several years, the house of representatives and senate were connected by a wooden walkway called the Cave of the Winds.

to adjust or add to the state's laws. The state's lawmakers and citizens vote on the amendments. The Kansas Constitution divides the state government into three branches: executive, legislative, and judicial.

THE EXECUTIVE BRANCH

The executive branch is responsible for making sure state laws are obeyed. The governor heads the executive branch. The governor is responsible for protecting the state's citizens and enforcing the laws. He or she oversees many agen-

The governor's mansion, Cedar Crest, is in MacLennan Park, a 244-acre (99 ha) park and wildlife refuge overlooking the Kansas River in Topeka.

cies and programs and also decides how much money the state can spend. The governor appoints judges to the Kansas Supreme Court and people to serve as the cabinet. Cabinet members advise the governor on different subjects, such as agriculture, transportation, and the environment.

If the governor dies or can no longer serve, the lieutenant governor becomes the new governor. Other top executive branch officials include the secretary of state, who oversees voting in the state; the state treasurer, who is in charge of collecting taxes and investing the state's money; and the attorney general, the state's top lawyer.

MINI-BIO

KATHLEEN SEBELIUS: GOVERNOR AND CABINET MEMBER

Kathleen Sebelius (1948–) was the second female governor of Kansas (the first was Joan Finney, who served from 1991 to 1995). She became governor in 2003 and was reelected in 2006. As governor, she focused on public education. In 2009, President Barack Obama nominated Sebelius for the position of secretary of health and human services. After being confirmed, she worked on creating the Affordable Care Act, also known as Obamacare, which aims to improve the quality of health care in America and make it more affordable for all citizens. She left the president's cabinet in 2014.

? **Want to know more?** Visit www.factsfornow .scholastic.com and enter the keyword **Kansas**.

Kansas State Government

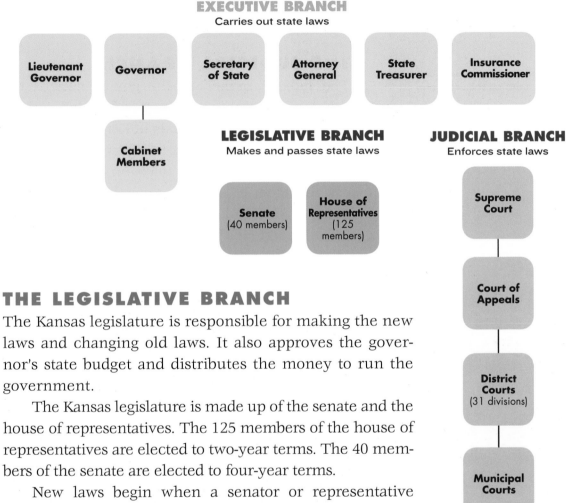

EXECUTIVE BRANCH
Carries out state laws

Lieutenant Governor

Governor

Secretary of State

Attorney General

State Treasurer

Insurance Commissioner

Cabinet Members

LEGISLATIVE BRANCH
Makes and passes state laws

Senate (40 members)

House of Representatives (125 members)

JUDICIAL BRANCH
Enforces state laws

Supreme Court

Court of Appeals

District Courts (31 divisions)

Municipal Courts

THE LEGISLATIVE BRANCH

The Kansas legislature is responsible for making the new laws and changing old laws. It also approves the governor's state budget and distributes the money to run the government.

The Kansas legislature is made up of the senate and the house of representatives. The 125 members of the house of representatives are elected to two-year terms. The 40 members of the senate are elected to four-year terms.

New laws begin when a senator or representative writes a bill. Both the house and the senate discuss and vote on the bill. If the legislature passes the bill, it is sent to the governor. If the governor signs the bill, it becomes a state law. The governor can also reject, or veto, the bill. If two-thirds of the members of both the senate and the house approve the bill again, their vote overrides the veto and the bill automatically becomes law.

The Kansas legislature meets every January for about 90 days. The Legislative Coordinating Council, which

Representing Kansas

This list shows the number of elected officials who represent Kansas, both on the state and national levels.

OFFICE	NUMBER	LENGTH OF TERM
State senators	40	4 years
State representatives	125	2 years
U.S. senators	2	6 years
U.S. representatives	4	2 years
Presidential electors	6	—

The Kansas Senate in session

meets monthly, is made up of three senators and four representatives. It acts for the legislature when it is not in session.

THE JUDICIAL BRANCH

The judicial branch of the government is the state's court system. Kansas is divided into 31 judicial districts. Most trials in Kansas are held in a district court. If a person thinks a mistake was made in a district court decision, he or she can ask the Kansas Court of Appeals to review the case. Thirteen judges sit on the court of appeals, although not all of them hear every case.

A Kansas legislative committee listens to a speaker discuss a reform plan for the state's health care system.

The Kansas Supreme Court reviews decisions by the court of appeals. The supreme court is the highest court in the state. Its decision is final. There are seven judges, or justices, in the Kansas Supreme Court. The judge who has served on the court for the longest time is the chief justice.

TEENS IN COURT

Kansas has teen courts, which are also called youth courts. These courts are run by young people. If there is a jury, its members are teenagers. If there is no jury, teen lawyers present the case to a panel of three teenage judges.

Kansas Counties

This map shows the 105 counties in Kansas. Topeka, the state capital, is indicated with a star.

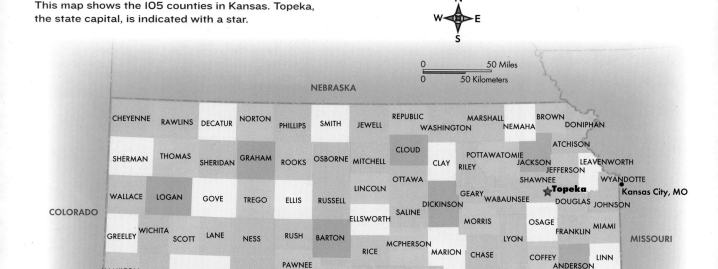

A person who is found guilty in teen court does not go to prison. Instead, the offender might have to write an apology to the person who was injured, spend time serving the community, or attend classes about drug and alcohol abuse.

The Kansas Bar Association sponsors another program that allows teenagers to learn about courts. Each year, the association holds a statewide competition for high school students in which teams of students prepare and present a case in a courtroom trial.

With help from the county clerk, a seventh-grader takes part in Kids Voting Kansas.

KIDS VOTING KANSAS

Fifty-five communities in Kansas take part in a program called Kids Voting Kansas. This program teaches kids—from elementary school through high school—about the voting process and the importance of voting. Kids go to the polls with their parents to "vote" for candidates and issues.

The kids' votes don't count in the actual election, but they are counted and reported in newspapers, on television, and on the organization's Web site. This program helps kids get involved in their state's and country's governments, so they grow up to be informed and active citizens.

KANSANS IN THE WHITE HOUSE

Dwight David Eisenhower (1890–1969) was the 34th president of the United States. He served two terms, from 1953 to 1961. He was born in Denison, Texas, and grew up in Abilene, Kansas. He served as the supreme Allied commander in Europe during World War II. Eisenhower's nickname was Ike, and during his 1952 campaign, people wore buttons that read "I like Ike."

Charles Curtis (1860–1936) was the 31st vice president of the United States. He served with President Herbert Hoover from 1929 to 1933. Curtis, who was part Kansa Indian, grew up on a Kaw reservation near Council Grove and spent much of his childhood in Topeka. He is the only person of Native American descent to hold such a high national office.

State Flag

Kansas's flag features the Great Seal of the State of Kansas on a blue background. The state crest, a sunflower resting on a twisted blue and gold bar, sits above the seal. The flag was adopted in 1927.

State Seal

The Great Seal of the State of Kansas depicts a river and a steamboat, representing commerce; a settler's cabin and a farmer plowing, representing agriculture; a wagon train heading west; a herd of bison; and two Native American hunters. The seal features the state motto, *Ad astra per aspera*, which is Latin for "To the stars through difficulties." It also includes 34 stars, representing Kansas as the 34th state, and the date of statehood.

READ ABOUT

A manufacturer works inside the body of an airplane at a factory in Wichita.

CHAPTER EIGHT

ECONOMY

★

KANSAS IS A GREAT PLACE TO LIVE—AND A GREAT PLACE TO WORK. Kansas workers have made their state one of the country's top producers of aircraft, wheat, flour, and helium. Bus drivers in Topeka, teachers in Olathe, and meatpackers in Garden City also contribute to the state's economy.

Teachers, like this one in Wichita, are among the many service workers who contribute to the Kansas economy.

Kansas produced about 277 million bushels of wheat in 2011. That's enough to make about 2 billion loaves of bread!

SERVICE INDUSTRIES

Most people in Kansas work in jobs that help other people. They work in education and in health and social services. Others work as bankers, store clerks, real estate agents, waiters, and insurance agents. The jobs of all these people are part of the state's service industries.

WHEAT AND MORE

Farming is big business in Kansas. The state has about 65,500 farms spread across the state. In 2011, Kansas exported roughly $5.3 billion worth of farm products. More than $1.5 billion came from the sale of wheat.

Kansas is the nation's second-biggest wheat-producing state, behind North Dakota. More than half of the wheat grown in Kansas is shipped to other countries. The rest stays in Kansas, where mills grind it into flour.

Corn is the state's second-largest crop. Kansas produced more than 453 million bushels of corn in 2011. Soybeans, another major crop, grow mostly in the eastern part of the state.

Kansas produces more than half of the nation's grain sorghum. Grain sorghum, which is also called milo, is a food for farm animals. Both corn and grain sorghum are also used to make ethanol. Ethanol is a car fuel that produces less pollution than traditional gasoline. Kansas has eight ethanol plants, and many more are being built.

One of Kansas's nicknames is the Sunflower State, so of course Kansas grows sunflowers, too. Sunflowers are

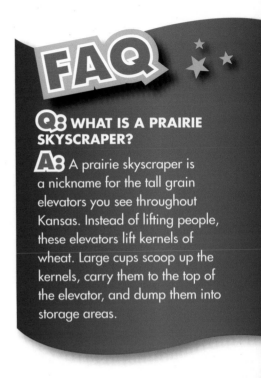

FAQ

Q8 WHAT IS A PRAIRIE SKYSCRAPER?

A8 A prairie skyscraper is a nickname for the tall grain elevators you see throughout Kansas. Instead of lifting people, these elevators lift kernels of wheat. Large cups scoop up the kernels, carry them to the top of the elevator, and dump them into storage areas.

Harvesting a field in Clearwater

Beef cattle grazing on a pasture in Garden City

made into sunflower oil, one of the world's most popular cooking oils. They also produce seeds, which make great snacks for both birds and people. In 2011, Kansas grew more than 149 million pounds (67 million kilograms) of sunflowers!

Beef cattle account for more than half the farm income in Kansas. In 2013, Kansas was the third-largest cattle-producing state in the country. The Flint Hills are filled with large ranches. Some Kansas farmers raise bison, or American buffalo, as a source of food, too. Kansas farmers also raise pigs, sheep, and other animals.

Southwestern Kansas is home to a huge concentration of meatpacking plants. A plant in Garden City is one of the largest in the world.

Major Agricultural and Mining Products

This map shows where Kansas's major agricultural and mining products come from. See a chicken? That means poultry is found there.

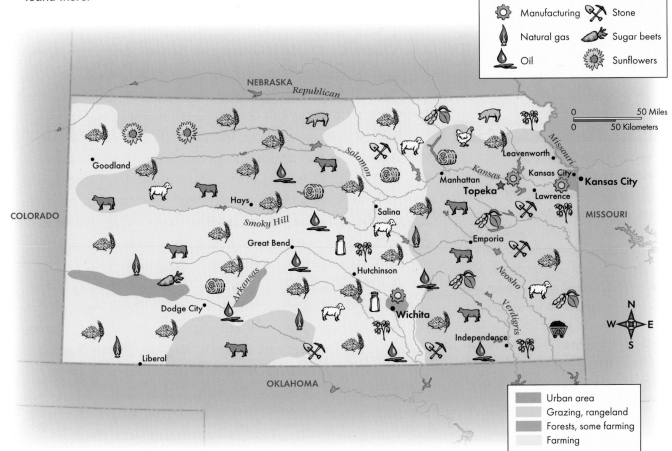

Legend:
- Cattle
- Coal
- Grains
- Hay
- Hogs
- Manufacturing
- Natural gas
- Oil
- Oats
- Poultry
- Salt
- Sheep
- Soybeans
- Stone
- Sugar beets
- Sunflowers

Urban area
Grazing, rangeland
Forests, some farming
Farming

BURIED TREASURES

In 1893, Kansas's first large oil well was dug near Neodesha. Kansas was the first western state to produce oil for fuel. In 2012, Kansas produced nearly 44 million barrels of oil.

Kansas has one of the world's largest natural supplies of helium. Helium is a gas that is lighter than air. During World War I, the U.S. Navy used Kansas helium to

Hutchinson, in south-central Kansas, has the world's largest salt deposit. It's about 100 miles (161 km) long and 40 miles (64 km) wide!

SEE IT HERE!

BIG BRUTUS

Today, only a few coal mines remain in Kansas, but for more than 100 years, coal mining was a major industry in the state. Big Brutus is one of the world's largest power shovels. For 12 years, it dug coal out of Mine 19, one of the many coal mines in southeastern Kansas. Big Brutus is 16 stories high and weighs 11 million pounds (5 million kg). It stopped digging in 1974. Today, Big Brutus is part of a museum in West Mineral dedicated to Kansas's coal-mining history.

fly dirigibles, or blimps, that hunted for German submarines. Today, helium is used in rockets, lasers, welding, and electronics. Helium is also mixed with oxygen in air tanks for deep-sea divers. People inflate party balloons with helium, too!

The Hugoton Gas Field is a major natural gas field in North America. It lies beneath southwestern Kansas and extends into Oklahoma and Texas. Since the early 2000s, the field has been producing less helium. Scientists believe much of it has already been removed, and they are working on ways to conserve what remains.

Salt mining is a major industry in Kansas. The state ranks fourth in the nation in salt production. There are salt mines in Hutchinson, Lyons, and Kanopolis. Limestone, which is used as a building material, is mined in eastern Kansas. Gypsum, another building material, is also mined in the state. Other important mining products in Kansas are sand, Portland cement, gravel, and clay.

For more than 100 years, coal mining was a big industry in Kansas. Today, coal still provides 74 percent of the state's electricity, but the state's only active coal mines are in Linn County, in eastern Kansas. Some Kansans have begun harnessing the power of the wind to produce electricity. They believe that wind is a better source of electricity than coal because it does not pollute the environment and there is an endless supply of wind.

Top Products

Crops Wheat, corn, soybeans, hay, grain sorghum, sunflowers

Livestock Cattle, hogs, pigs

Mining Petroleum, natural gas, helium, gypsum, limestone, salt, Portland cement, crushed stone and gravel, sand, clay

Manufacturing Transportation equipment (aircraft, automobiles, railroad cars, locomotives), processed foods, printed materials, chemicals, rubber and plastic products, electronic equipment

HIGH-FLYING WICHITA

Kansas leads the nation in the making of aircraft. Kansas's aircraft industry, which is centered in

THINK ABOUT IT!

Wind Power

PRO

Many Kansans believe the state should build wind farms to produce energy. Wind farms consist of tall windmills. The whirling blades on the windmills run generators that produce electricity. People in favor of wind power point out that there is an endless supply of wind. Also, wind does not pollute the environment like burning coal does. They say the state could decide where wind farms are built so that they would not disturb nature preserves. Governor Kathleen Sebelius supports using wind power. She has said, "Quite simply, we have a moral obligation to be good stewards of this state, because we are only here for a short time and we will ultimately pass it on to our children."

CON

Other people question whether wind power is a good idea. Wind power is more expensive to produce than other types of electricity, and birds sometimes get killed in the spinning blades of the wind towers. State representative Frank Miller believes that the 35-story wind towers would spoil the beauty of the tallgrass prairies, now enjoyed by state residents and thousands of tourists each year. He says, "The bulk of the windmills become an eyesore in many scenic areas, may affect bird migration, and potentially would adversely impact ecological rarities such as the Flint Hills of Kansas."

Wind turbines

Wichita, is the largest employer in the state. Many jobs in Kansas's **aviation** industry were lost in the wake of the 2007–2008 worldwide financial crisis. Still, in 2013, about 30,300 Kansans worked in aviation.

Kansas has a number of major aircraft companies: Airbus/North American Wing Design, Boeing, Bombardier Aerospace/Learjet, Cessna, Hawker Beechcraft, Spirit AeroSystems, and Raytheon. Many of these companies also work with the National Aeronautics and Space Administration (NASA) to develop new technology for the space program.

WORD TO KNOW

aviation *the design and manufacture of airplanes*

MINI-BIO

WILLIAM C. COLEMAN: INVENTOR

The Coleman Company, owned by William Coleman (1870–1957), began making lamps in Wichita in 1905. During World War II, the U.S. Army asked the company to design a portable stove, so soldiers could heat food and water. In response, the company created the G-1 Pocket Stove. Soldiers carried the stove during the war, and Coleman was soon selling the Pocket Stove to hunters and campers back home. In 1990, Coleman was elected to Emporia State University's Kansas Business Hall of Fame.

? Want to know more? Visit www.factsfornow .scholastic.com and enter the keyword **Kansas**.

MADE IN KANSAS

General Motors makes cars in its Fairfax plant in Kansas City, which employs about 3,900 people. The company claims that workers produce a new car every 58 seconds. General Motors is one of the

A baker prepares dough at Wheatfields Bakery in Lawrence.

largest manufacturers of the flexible-fuel vehicle, a type of car that runs with a mix of gasoline and ethanol fuel.

Goodyear Tire & Rubber Company employs about 1,550 Kansans at its plant in Topeka. Another major employer in Kansas is the Coleman Company, a world-wide leader in camping gear.

A veterinarian named Mark Morris founded Hill's Pet Nutrition in Topeka in 1948. Today, the company is a world leader in producing healthy foods for cats and dogs. The company has veterinarians on staff worldwide, making it one of the largest employers of veterinarians in the world.

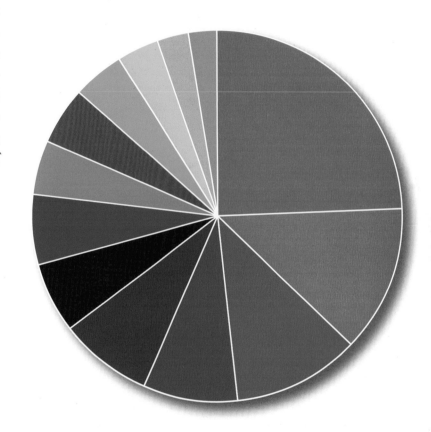

What Do Kansans Do?

This color-coded chart shows what industries Kansans work in.

24.5% Educational services, and health care and social assistance 341,871

12.9% Manufacturing 179,685

11.2% Retail trade 156,320

8.4% Professional, scientific, and management, and administrative and waste management services 117,261

7.8% Arts, entertainment, and recreation, and accommodation and food services 108,752

6.3% Construction 88,243

6.1% Finance and insurance, and real estate and rental and leasing 84,583

4.8% Public administration 67,200

4.8% Transportation and warehousing, and utilities 66,797

4.6% Other services, except public administration 64,074

3.5% Agriculture, forestry, fishing and hunting, and mining 48,741

2.8% Wholesale trade 39,154

2.4% Information 32,953

Source: U.S. Census Bureau, 2010 census

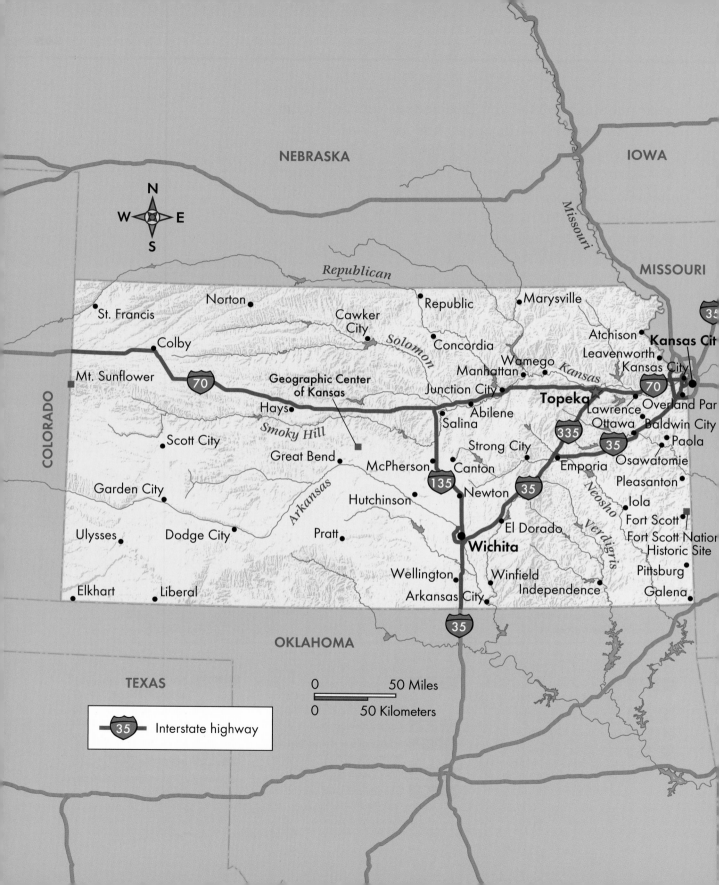

TRAVEL GUIDE

★

From the very top of Mount Sunflower to the bottom of the Verdigris River Basin, Kansas will surprise you! As you travel across the state, you'll see the world's largest ball of twine and a bit of the yellow brick road. You can visit the Kansas Cosmosphere and Space Center and the Flint Hills tallgrass prairie. There's a lot to see and do in Kansas, so grab your map and let's go!

←—Follow along with this travel map. We'll begin in Kansas City and travel all the way west to Dodge City!

NORTHEAST

THINGS TO DO: Go on a scavenger hunt, get a T-shirt signed by your favorite NASCAR driver, and take an old-fashioned train to Nowhere.

Kansas City

★ **Kansas Speedway:** Check out the fast-paced action on this 1.5-mile (2 km) track, home to NASCAR racing championships since 2001. The Fan Walk lets you get behind the scenes at ground level, so you can watch the crew work and ask them questions.

★ **Kansas City 18th & Vine Jazz & Blues Festival:** Kansas City is the home of blues and jazz—and the birthplace of legendary saxophonist Charlie "Bird" Parker. Each year, music greats show up for this festival.

Kansas Speedway

SEE IT HERE!

STRAWBERRY HILL MUSEUM AND CULTURAL CENTER

You'll feel as if you're in eastern Europe when you visit this museum in the heart of Strawberry Hill, a Kansas City neighborhood settled by people from Croatia and Slovenia in the 1800s. You'll find jewelry, costumes, hand-carved dolls, and toys from those countries, as well as from Ukraine, Poland, Russia, and others. Photographers and artists who grew up in the neighborhood often have artwork on display.

Baldwin City

★ **Train to Nowhere:** Hop the Midland Rail in Baldwin City and head off for your final destination—Nowhere. That's the name of the official stop along this scenic train trip to Ottawa. The railroad line was built in 1867 and leaves from an old depot of the Santa Fe railroad. Along the way, you'll see ruins of a mission built in 1857 and other historic sites.

Overland Park

★ **Overland Park Arboretum and Botanical Gardens:** This garden includes a variety of environments, including prairie grasses, waterfalls, and thick forests. You can go on a scavenger hunt, climb the Sky Watch (a spiral walkway to a lookout point), or wander miles of hiking trails.

Brown v. Board of Education National Historic Site

Topeka

★ **Brown v. Board of Education National Historic Site:** At this museum, you can learn all about the U.S. Supreme Court decision that ended school segregation.

NORTH CENTRAL

THINGS TO DO: Eat chocolates in Abilene, see rare animals, and tour the boyhood home of the 34th president.

Abilene

★ **Dwight D. Eisenhower Presidential Library, Museum, and Boyhood Home:** This center preserves the family home of President Dwight D. Eisenhower. The presidential library contains around 26 million pages of the president's documents.

★ **Russell Stover Candies Factory:** Here you can munch on free samples while you're watching the candy makers at work. This is one of the few candy companies that still dips its chocolate-covered cherries by hand!

Statue at the Eisenhower Presidential Library

The Oz Museum

Wamego

★ **The Oz Museum:** This museum holds the world's largest collection of items related to Dorothy's trip from Kansas to the Land of Oz in *The Wizard of Oz*. You can see more than 2,000 posters, puzzles, games, and toys—and statues of all the characters.

Salina

★ **Rolling Hills Zoo:** At this zoo, you can get up close and personal with a white camel, a snow leopard, a rhinoceros, an aardvark, an orangutan, and a giraffe, too. You can also take a tram ride through the rolling prairie. A museum includes a 3-D movie theater and talking, moving robots.

NORTHWEST

THINGS TO DO: Visit a Native American earth lodge and see a fish within a fish—even if you don't have X-ray vision!

Hays

★ **Sternberg Museum of Natural History:** On a visit to this museum, you'll travel back in time millions of years, to when giant sea creatures swam in the oceans that covered Kansas. You'll find giant growling dinosaurs, a mammoth skeleton, and prehistoric birds. Don't miss the fish within a fish—one of the state's oldest fossils, known as the "Fish-Within-A-Fish". Bones of a little fish are still inside the bones of the fish that ate it!

Republic

★ **Pawnee Indian Museum State Historic Site:** This museum is built around the floor of an earth lodge, where Pawnees lived more than 200 years ago.

SEE IT HERE!

CASTLE ROCK AND MONUMENT ROCKS

Giant chalk formations rise from the ground in Gove, Scott, Logan, and Lane counties. These fragile structures are traces of the ancient sea that once covered the land. Castle Rock is almost 70 feet (21 m) high. Nearby are the Monument Rocks, which are filled with fossils of fish— even sharks!

THE WORLD'S LARGEST BALL OF TWINE

On Wisconsin Street in downtown Cawker City, there's a ball of twine that weighs almost 10 tons. Frank Stoeber started the ball from scraps of twine in 1953. When he gave it to the town, it already weighed 5,000 pounds (2,270 kg). The townspeople have been adding to it ever since. Every August, at an annual event called a Twine-a-Thon, citizens and visitors take turns wrapping twine on the ball.

SOUTHEAST

THINGS TO DO: Dress up for a Neewollah masquerade ball, ride a carousel, and visit a pioneer home.

Independence

★ **Little House on the Prairie Museum:** This one-room cabin marks the spot where children's book author Laura Ingalls Wilder and her family once lived. Her book, *Little House on the Prairie*, and the television series of the same name have made this part of Kansas famous.

★ **Neewollah Festival:** In case you were wondering, that's Halloween spelled backward! Independence has been celebrating the season in its own way since 1919. The nine-day festival includes a carnival, parades, a masquerade ball, the Great Pumpkin Contest, a chili cook-off, marching bands, and live music.

★ **Riverside Park:** It costs only five cents to ride the carousel at this amusement park. There's also a miniature train, a miniature golf course, swimming pools, and playgrounds. Bears, cougars, and monkeys live at the zoo, which was home to Miss Able, the first monkey in outer space.

Pleasanton

★ **Marais des Cygnes National Wildlife Refuge:** Hundreds of thousands of birds pass through here as they travel during the fall and spring seasons. You might see ducks, geese, herons, pelicans, and shorebirds. Visitors can also pick wild strawberries, blackberries, mushrooms, walnuts, and pecans from the bushes and trees in the area. There are plenty of fishing spots, too.

Sandhill crane

SEE IT HERE!

FORT SCOTT NATIONAL HISTORIC SITE

The U.S. Army built this fort in 1842 to keep peace between settlers and Native Americans and to protect travelers and traders on the Santa Fe trail. In the days of the Civil War, the fort was a supply and training center. Today, the site features 20 historic structures. During special events, you'll see people dressed in historical costumes or riding on horseback. You can also take part in old-fashioned games, such as tug-of-war and sack races.

Osawatomie

★ **John Brown Memorial Park:** John Brown fought slavery to make Kansas a Free State. The log cabin in this park's museum was the home of his half sister, Florella, and her husband, the Reverend Samuel Adair, and is where Brown often stayed. Nearby is the site of the famous Battle of Osawatomie. There's a monument at the battle site and a life-size statue of John Brown in the park.

John Brown monument

SOUTH CENTRAL

THINGS TO DO: See trophies won by talented Kansas athletes, watch bareback riders at the Flint Hills Rodeo, and take a tram ride through the Maxwell Wildlife Refuge.

Canton

★ **Maxwell Wildlife Refuge:** Around 200 American buffalo graze on the 2,800 acres (1,133 ha) of this nature preserve in the Flint Hills. Get a bird's-eye view from the observation tower or take the guided tour riding in an open tram. You'll also see elk, native flowers, wild grasses, and other Kansas plants and wildlife.

Buffalo at the Maxwell Wildlife Refuge

Displays at the Kansas Sports Hall of Fame

Wichita

★ **Kansas Sports Hall of Fame:**
Learn all about the Kansas greats
of the sports world—major league
pitcher Walter Johnson, basketball stars Wilt Chamberlain and
Lynette Woodard, running back Gale
Sayers, and others. The museum
displays hundreds of jerseys, bas-
ketballs, helmets, bats, trophies, and
photographs.

Strong City

★ **Flint Hills Rodeo:** This is the
oldest rodeo in Kansas. Every June,
cowboys and cowgirls compete in
six events for championship prizes.
Barrel racing, bareback riding,
cowboy dances, rodeo parades, and
other special events are part of the
rodeo, too.

SEE IT HERE!

THE MID-AMERICA
ALL-INDIAN CENTER

The Mid-America All-Indian Center in Wichita
is a living museum that looks and sounds like
a Native American village of the 1850s. The
center also shows works by contemporary Native
American artists, such as Woody Crumbo,
Blackbear Bosin, and Jerome Tiger. The Gallery
of Nations displays the flags of each of the 549
Native American nations recognized by the
U.S. government. A powwow, with traditional
dancing, drumming, and singing, takes place
every year. The center also offers classes in
beadwork and other Native American crafts.

SOUTHWEST

THINGS TO DO: Visit the wildest town in the Wild West, head into outer space at the Kansas Cosmosphere and Space Center, and walk along Liberal's own yellow brick road.

Hutchinson

★ **Kansas Cosmosphere and Space Center:** Blast off! This museum has the second-largest collection of space artifacts in the country. There's a full-size replica of the space shuttle *Endeavour*, the *Apollo 13* command module *Odyssey*, a moon rock from the *Apollo 11* mission, and the world's largest collection of space suits worn by astronauts. There are also star shows, laser light shows, and a live science show about rocket engines.

The *Endeavour* exhibit at the Kansas Cosmosphere and Space Center

Elkhart

★ **Cimarron National Grasslands:** This 108,000-acre (43,700 ha) grassland prairie is the largest area of public land in the state. You can drive through part of it, where you'll see antelope, deer, elk, prairie chickens, and a prairie dog town. Along the way, you'll also see traces of the Santa Fe Trail, which ran along the Cimarron River.

Liberal

★ **Dorothy's House and the Land of Oz:** In the movie *The Wizard of Oz*, the character Dorothy couldn't wait to get back to her home in Kansas. Here it is! Dorothy's House is an exact replica of the movie's version of the young girl's home—complete with witch's feet underneath! Outside you'll find a miniature yellow brick road, talking trees, flying monkeys, Munchkins, the Tin Man, the Scarecrow, the Cowardly Lion, and Toto, too.

★ **Mid-America Air Museum:** This museum has more than 100 aircraft, including military aircraft, helicopters, and hang gliders. Kids ages 8 to 12 can attend summer camp at Camp Falcon, where they make models and conduct test flights.

SEE IT HERE!

THE INTERNATIONAL PANCAKE DERBY

Every year, a group of women in Liberal run a 0.25-mile (0.4 km) race. What's unusual about that? Well, while they are running, they are also flipping pancakes. On the very same day, women in Olney, England, also run a pancake race. The winner's time in Liberal is compared to the winner's time in Olney.

A mural of the International Pancake Derby in Liberal

Front Street at the Boot Hill Museum

Dodge City

★ **Boot Hill Museum and the Gunfighters Wax Museum:** This village museum re-creates Front Street, the main street of old Dodge City, one of the wildest towns in the Wild West. You can see a general store, a blacksmith shop, the Fort Dodge jail, and more. Cowboys and townspeople in costumes provide living-history entertainment.

WRITING PROJECTS

Check out these ideas for creating campaign brochures and writing you-are-there editorials. Or learn about early explorers and settlers in the state.

118

ART PROJECTS

Create a great PowerPoint presentation, illustrate the state song, or learn about the state quarter and design your own.

119

TIMELINE

What happened when? This timeline highlights important events in the state's history—and shows what was happening throughout the United States at the same time.

122

FAST FACTS

Use this section to find fascinating facts about state symbols, land area and population statistics, weather, sports teams, and much more.

126

GLOSSARY

Remember the Words to Know from the chapters in this book? They're all collected here.

125

WRITING PROJECTS

Write a Memoir, Journal, or Editorial for Your School Newspaper!

Picture Yourself . . .

★ Coming of age in a Kansa village. Write journal entries describing your thoughts and preparations in the days leading to this event. Then tell what it's like to become an adult member of your community.

SEE: Chapter Two, pages 28–32.

★ Taking part in the civil rights movement. Write an editorial for your school newspaper about the struggles of various individuals and organizations in the movement, including the NAACP and parents such as Oliver Brown, who worked to ensure equal education for his daughter Linda and other African American children.

SEE: Chapter Five, pages 67–68.

Linda Brown and her class

Create an Election Brochure or Web Site!

Run for office!

Pretend you are a candidate for governor of Kansas and create a campaign brochure or Web site. Explain how you meet the qualifications to be governor, and talk about the three or four major issues you'll focus on if you are elected. Remember, you'll be responsible for the state budget. How do you propose to spend the taxpayers' money?

SEE: Chapter Seven, pages 86–93.

Compare and Contrast —When, Why, and How Did They Come?

Compare the migrations and explorations of the first Native people in Kansas and the region's first European explorers. Tell about:

★ When their migrations began
★ How they traveled
★ Why they migrated
★ Where their journeys began and ended
★ What they found when they arrived

SEE: Chapters Two and Three, pages 26–41.

ART PROJECTS

Create a PowerPoint Presentation or Visitors' Guide

Welcome to Kansas!

Kansas is a great place to visit—and to live! From its natural beauty to its bustling cities and historic sites, there's plenty to see and do. In your PowerPoint presentation or brochure, highlight 10 to 15 of Kansas's amazing landmarks. Be sure to include:

★ a map of the state locating these sites

★ photos, illustrations, Web links, natural history facts, geographic stats, climate and weather info, and descriptions of plants and wildlife

> **SEE:** Chapter Nine, pages 107–115, and Fast Facts, pages 126–127.

Illustrate the Lyrics to the Kansas State Song

("Home on the Range")

Use markers, paints, photos, collages, colored pencils, or computer graphics to illustrate the lyrics to "Home on the Range," the state song. Turn your illustrations into a picture book, or scan them into a PowerPoint presentation and add music!

> **SEE:** The lyrics to "Home on the Range" on page 128.

Research Kansas's State Quarter

From 1999 to 2008, the U.S. Mint introduced new quarters commemorating each of the 50 states in the order that they were admitted to the Union. Each state's quarter features a unique design on its reverse, or back.

★ Research the significance of the image. Who designed the quarter? Who chose the final design?

★ Design your own Kansas quarter. What images would you choose for the reverse?

★ Make a poster showing the Kansas quarter and label each image.

GO TO: www.factsfornow.scholastic.com. Enter the keyword **Kansas** and look for the link to the Kansas quarter.

SCIENCE, TECHNOLOGY, ENGINEERING, & MATH PROJECTS

Graph Population Statistics!

★ Compare population statistics (such as ethnic background, birth, death, and literacy rates) in Kansas counties or major cities.

★ Look at population densities and write sentences describing what the population statistics show; graph one set of population statistics and write a paragraph explaining what the graphs reveal.

SEE: Chapter Six, pages 72–77.

Create a Weather Map of Kansas!

Use your knowledge of Kansas's geography to research and identify conditions that result in specific weather events. How does the geography of Kansas make it vulnerable to tornadoes? Create a weather map or poster that shows the state's weather patterns. Include a caption explaining the technology used to measure weather phenomena.

SEE: Chapter One, pages 11–18.

Track Endangered Species

★ Using your knowledge of Kansas's wildlife, research what animals and plants are endangered or threatened. Find out what the state is doing to protect these species. Chart known populations of the animals and plants, and report on changes in certain geographic areas.

SEE: Chapter One, pages 19–22.

Greater prairie chicken

PRIMARY VS. SECONDARY SOURCES

What's the Diff?

Your teacher may require at least one or two primary sources and one or two secondary sources for your assignment. So, what's the difference between the two?

★ **Primary sources are original.** You are reading the actual words of someone's diary, journal, letter, autobiography, or interview. Primary sources can also be photographs, maps, prints, cartoons, news/film footage, posters, first-person newspaper articles, drawings, musical scores, and recordings. By the way, when you conduct a survey, interview someone, shoot a video, or take photographs to include in a project, you are creating primary sources!

★ **Secondary sources are what you find in encyclopedias, textbooks, articles, biographies, and almanacs.** These are written by a person or group of people who tell about something that happened to someone else. Secondary sources also recount what another person said or did. This book is an example of a secondary source.

Now that you know what primary sources are—where can you find them?

★ **Your school or local library:** Check the library catalog for collections of original writings, government documents, musical scores, and so on. Some of this material may be stored on microfilm.

★ **Historical societies:** These organizations keep historical documents, photographs, and other materials. Staff members can help you find what you are looking for. History museums are also great places to see primary sources firsthand.

★ **The Internet:** There are lots of sites that have primary sources you can download and use in a project or assignment.

TIMELINE

★ ★ ★

U.S. Events `1500` **Kansas Events**

1500s
Kansa, Pawnee, Wichita, Osage, and other groups live in what is now Kansas.

1541
Spanish explorer Francisco Vásquez de Coronado enters what is now Kansas.

`1600`

1565
Spanish admiral Pedro Menéndez de Avilés founds St. Augustine, Florida, the oldest continuously occupied European settlement in the continental United States.

1673
French explorers Louis Jolliet and Jacques Marquette draw the first maps to show parts of Kansas.

1682
René-Robert Cavelier, Sieur de La Salle, claims more than 1 million square miles (2.6 million sq km) of territory in the Mississippi River basin for France, naming it Louisiana.

1682
French explorer René-Robert Cavelier, Sieur de La Salle, claims Louisiana, which includes Kansas, for France.

`1700`

c. 1700
Native Americans on the Great Plains acquire horses.

1744
Fort de Cavagnial becomes the first European settlement in Kansas.

1754–63
England and France fight over North American colonial lands in the French and Indian War. By the end of the war, France cedes all of its land west of the Mississippi to Spain and its Canadian territories to England.

1776
Thirteen American colonies declare their independence from Great Britain.

Trading between Europeans and Native Americans

U.S. Events | 1800 | Kansas Events

1803
The Louisiana Purchase almost doubles the size of the United States.

1803
The United States purchases the Louisiana territory, which includes most of Kansas.

1812–15
The United States and Great Britain fight the War of 1812.

1821
William Becknell opens the Santa Fe Trail.

1830
The Indian Removal Act forces eastern Native American groups to relocate west of the Mississippi River.

1830
Native American groups from the East are forced to Kansas Territory and other regions west of the Mississippi River.

1854
The Kansas-Nebraska Act allows Kansas residents to decide about slavery.

1859
Free Staters draft the Wyandotte Constitution.

1861–65
The American Civil War is fought between the Northern Union and the Southern Confederacy; it ends with the surrender of the Confederate army, led by General Robert E. Lee.

1861
Kansas becomes the 34th state.

1864
Union forces win the Battle of Mine Creek, the only Civil War battle to take place in Kansas.

1866
The U.S. Congress approves the Fourteenth Amendment to the U.S. Constitution, granting citizenship to African Americans.

1879
Thousands of African Americans called exodusters migrate to Kansas.

1887
Susanna M. Salter is elected mayor of Argonia, becoming the first female mayor in the United States.

U.S. Events `1900` **Kansas Events**

1912
Women in Kansas gain the right
to vote in all elections.

1917–18
The United States engages in World War I.

1920s
Kansas's aircraft industry flourishes.

1929
The stock market crashes, plunging
the United States more deeply
into the Great Depression.

1930s
Severe drought produces huge
dust storms across Kansas.

1941–45
The United States engages in World War II.

1951
Flooding in eastern Kansas damages or
destroys 45,000 homes in Kansas.

1954
The U.S. Supreme Court prohibits
segregation of public schools in the *Brown
v. Board of Education of Topeka* ruling.

1954
The U.S. Supreme Court rules that
school segregation is illegal in *Brown
v. Board of Education of Topeka*.

1956
The Kansas Turnpike opens.

1964–73
The United States engages
in the Vietnam War.

1970
Nearly two-thirds of Kansans live in cities.

1990
Joan Finney is elected the first
female governor of Kansas.

1991
The United States and other nations engage
in the brief Persian Gulf War against Iraq.

`2000`

2001
Terrorists hijack four U.S. aircraft and crash
them into the World Trade Center in New
York City, the Pentagon in Arlington, Virginia,
and a Pennsylvania field, killing thousands.

2005
Time magazine names
Kathleen Sebelius one of the
nation's five best governors.

Kathleen Sebelius

2014
Former governor Kathleen Sebelius resigns as
U.S. secretary of health and human services.

GLOSSARY

allies people who are on the same side in a conflict

amendment a change to a law or legal document

aviation the design and manufacture of airplanes

breechcloths garments worn by men over their lower bodies

cavalry soldiers who ride on horseback

ceded gave up or granted

constitution a written document that contains all the governing principles of a state or country

corps a group working together on a special mission

editorials newspaper articles that give the opinion of a paper's editor or publisher

extinct no longer existing

foreclosures legal processes for taking back property when the payment for it is overdue

fossils the remains or prints of ancient animals or plants left in stone

geologists scientists who study the history of Earth

glaciers slow-moving masses of ice

guerrillas soldiers who don't belong to regular armies; they often use surprise attacks and other uncommon battle tactics

irrigation watering land by artificial means to promote plant growth

migration movement from one place to another

missionaries people who try to convert others to a religion

plantation a large farm that grows mainly one crop

pueblo a flat-roofed house, usually made from dried mud and straw, built by Native Americans of the desert Southwest; also, a community of these houses

sedimentary formed from clay, sand, and gravel that settled at the bottom of a body of water

segregation separation from others according to race, class, ethnic group, religion, or other factors

sod soil thickly packed together with grass and roots

suffrage the right to vote

treaties written agreements between two or more groups

FAST FACTS

★ ★ ★

State Symbols

Statehood date	January 29, 1861, the 34th state
Origin of state name	Kaw word meaning "people of the south wind"
State capital	Topeka
State nickname	Sunflower State, Wheat State, Jayhawk State, Midway USA
State motto	*Ad astra per aspera* ("To the stars through difficulties")
State bird	Western meadowlark
State flower	Wild native sunflower
State animal	American buffalo
State insect	Honeybee
State song	"Home on the Range " (See lyrics on page 128)
State tree	Cottonwood
State reptile	Ornate box turtle
State amphibian	Barred tiger salamander
State fair	Mid-September at Hutchinson

State seal

Geography

Total area; rank	82,278 square miles (213,101 sq km); 15th
Land; rank	81,762 square miles (211,764 sq km); 13th
Water; rank	516 square miles (1,336 sq km); 42nd
Inland water; rank	516 square miles (1,336 sq km); 35th
Geographic center	Rice County, about 1.5 miles (2.4 km) southeast of Bushton
Latitude	37° N to 40° N
Longitude	94°38' W to 102°1'34" W
Highest point	Mount Sunflower, 4,039 feet (1,231 m)
Lowest point	Verdigris River, 679 feet (207 m)
Largest city	Wichita
Number of counties	105
Longest river	Arkansas River

Population

Population; rank (2010 census)	2,885,905; 33rd
Density (2010 census)	35 persons per square mile (14 per sq km)
Population distribution (2010 census)	74% urban, 26% rural
Ethnic distribution (2010 census)	White persons: 78.2%
	Persons of Hispanic or Latino origin: 10.5%
	Black persons: 5.7%
	Persons reporting two or more races: 2.3%
	Asian persons: 2.3%
	American Indian and Alaska Native persons: 0.8%
	Native Hawaiian and other Pacific Islanders: 0.1%
	People of some other race: 0.1%

Weather

Record high temperature	121°F (49°C) at Fredonia on July 18, 1936, and at Alton on July 24, 1936
Record low temperature	–40°F (–40°C) at Lebanon on February 13, 1905
Average July temperature, Wichita	81°F (27°C)
Average January temperature, Wichita	32°F (0°C)
Average annual precipitation, Wichita	33 inches (84 cm)

State flag

STATE SONG

★ ★ ★

"Home on the Range" (originally "My Western Home")

"Home on the Range" was officially adopted as the state song in 1947. Brewster Higley, a frontier doctor and homesteader in Smith County, wrote the lyrics. His original poem was published in the Smith County newspaper, the *Pioneer*, in December 1873, and the words have been slightly altered since then. Daniel Kelley, a member of a popular musical group in nearby Gaylord, wrote the music.

Oh, give me a home where the buffalo roam,
Where the deer and the antelope play,
Where seldom is heard a discouraging word
And the skies are not cloudy all day.

Chorus:
Home, home on the range
Where the deer and the antelope play,
Where seldom is heard a discouraging word
And the skies are not cloudy all day.

Where the air is so pure, the zephyrs so free,
The breezes so balmy and light
That I would not exchange my home on the range
For all of the cities so bright.
(Chorus)
How often at night when the heavens are bright
With the light from the glittering stars,
Have I stood here amazed and asked as I gazed
If their glory exceeds that of ours.

(Chorus)
Oh, I love these wild flowers in this dear land of ours,
The curlew I love to hear scream,
And I love the white rocks and the antelope flocks
That graze on the mountain-tops green.
(Chorus)
Oh, give me a land where the bright diamond sand
Flows leisurely down the stream,
Where the graceful white swan goes gliding along
Like a maid in a heavenly dream.
(Chorus)
Then I would not exchange my home on the range,
Where the deer and the antelope play,
Where seldom is heard a discouraging word
And the skies are not cloudy all day.

NATURAL AREAS AND HISTORIC SITES

National Historic Sites

Brown v. Board of Education National Historic Site commemorates the Supreme Court decision that led to the end of racial segregation in American schools. The site is the Monroe Elementary School, which Linda Brown attended.

Fort Larned National Historic Site preserves a military outpost built midway along the Santa Fe Trail to protect travelers and mail.

Fort Scott National Historic Site preserves a 19th-century frontier military base.

Nicodemus National Historic Site is the only remaining Kansas town established by African Americans at the end of Reconstruction.

National Trails

Freedom's Frontier National Heritage Area, located on the Kansas–Missouri border, features museums and historic sites that relate to slavery and other important issues of the 1800s.

Pioneers and gold miners journeyed across the *California National Trail*. Part of this trail runs through Kansas.

The *Lewis & Clark National Historic Trail* is the route traveled by Lewis and Clark on their voyage of discovery.

The *Oregon National Historic Trail* extends more than 2,000 miles (3,200 km) through parts of Missouri, Kansas, Nebraska, Wyoming, Idaho, and Oregon.

The *Pony Express National Historic Trail* follows the route of the Pony Express. The riders for the Pony Express traveled through eight states delivering and picking up mail.

The *Santa Fe National Historic Trail* was a trade route connecting Missouri and New Mexico.

National Preserves

The *Tallgrass Prairie National Preserve* protects almost 11,000 acres (4,500 ha) of prairie, along with a ranch house and a one-room schoolhouse.

State Parks

Kansas maintains 25 state parks and recreation areas, including El Dorado, Kanopolis, and Cedar Bluff.

SPORTS TEAMS

★ ★ ★

NCAA Teams (Division I)

Kansas State University *Wildcats*
University of Kansas *Jayhawks*
Wichita State University *Shockers*

Mario Chalmers puts up a three-point shot to send the Kansas Jayhawks to overtime in their 2008 NCAA Championship win over the University of Memphis.

CULTURAL INSTITUTIONS

Libraries

The *Kansas State Library* in Topeka provides information on the Kansas state government to the general public and public officials.

The *Kansas State Historical Society* has extensive materials on Kansas history and holds one of the nation's largest state newspaper collections.

Museums

The *University of Kansas Natural History Museum* (Lawrence) displays fossils of plants and animals that lived in the region long ago.

The *Smoky Hill Museum* (Salina) features more than 20,000 artifacts from the 1800s to the present day.

The *Kansas Museum of History* (Topeka) highlights eras from the state's past to the present with exhibits about Native American history, settlement, and railroads.

Performing Arts

The *Kansas City Symphony* was formed in 1911. Each year it puts on concerts, educational shows, and regional and national tours.

The *Wichita Grand Opera* stages classical opera and ballet performances.

Universities and Colleges

In 2011, Kansas had 8 public and 27 private institutions of higher education.

Haskell Indian Nations University

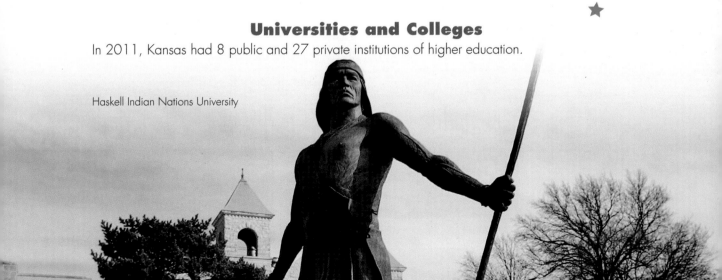

ANNUAL EVENTS

January–March

Kansas Day, statewide (January 29)

Cuba Rock-A-Thon in Cuba (March)

International Pancake Day in Liberal (Shrove Tuesday)

April–June

Civil War Encampment at Fort Scott (April)

Mennonite Relief Sale in Hutchinson (April)

Chisholm Trail Festival and Rodeo in Caldwell (May)

Santa Fe Trail Days in Larned (May)

Wichita River Festival in Wichita (May)

Beef Empire Days in Garden City (June)

Flint Hills Rodeo in Strong City (June)

Grassland Heritage Festival in Elkhart (June)

Midsummer's Day Festival in Lindsborg (June)

Prairie Band Potawatomi Annual Pow Wow in Mayetta (June)

Smoky Hill River Festival in Salina (June)

Symphony in the Flint Hills (June)

July–September

Amelia Earhart Festival in Atchison (July)

Days of '49 in Hanover (July)

Fiesta Mexicana in Topeka (July)

Czech Festival and Arts and Crafts Show in Wilson (late July)

Dodge City Days (late July)

Kickapoo Indian Pow Wow in Topeka (late July)

Emancipation Celebration in Nicodemus (July–August)

Flint Hills Beef Fest in Emporia (August)

Ellsworth Cowtown Festival in Ellsworth (August)

Pony Express Festival in Hanover (August)

State Fiddling & Picking Championships in Lawrence (August)

Kansas State Fair in Hutchinson (mid-September)

Historic Fort Hays Days in Hays (September)

October–December

Wild Wild West in Olathe (October)

Pioneer Christmas Arts and Crafts Festival in Wichita (November)

Trail of Lights in Great Bend (November and December)

St. Lucia Festival in Lindsborg (December)

BIOGRAPHICAL DICTIONARY

Kirstie Alley (1951–) is an actress who was born in Wichita. She is best known for her role as Rebecca Howe in the TV series *Cheers* from 1987 to 1993. She has also written two books.

Annette Bening (1958–) is an award-winning film and television actor who was born in Topeka. She has starred in such films as *Bugsy*, *Regarding Henry*, and *Being Julia*.

Blackbear Bosin See page 32.

Erin Brockovich (1960–) was born in Lawrence and attended Kansas State University at Manhattan. As a legal clerk, she helped to prepare a case against a large company that was accused of polluting the water in a town in California. Julia Roberts starred in a film about the case in 2000, titled *Erin Brockovich*.

Gwendolyn Brooks (1917–2000) was a poet born in Topeka. She published her first poem when she was 13 and later became the first African American to receive a Pulitzer Prize.

Annette Bening

Louise Brooks (1906–1985) was an actress and dancer who gained fame in the early years of Hollywood movies. She was born in Cherryvale.

John Brown (1800–1859) was an abolitionist, a person who strongly opposed slavery. He fought proslavery supporters in wars along the Kansas–Missouri border, and in 1859, led an unsuccessful raid on a U.S. government weapons post at Harpers Ferry, Virginia.

William Burroughs (1914–1997) was an influential writer and one of the main members of what is known as the Beat Generation. His best-known novel is *Naked Lunch* (1959), which follows the life of a drug abuser. Born in St. Louis, Missouri, Burroughs lived in Lawrence for many years.

Dan Carney (1931–) and Frank Carney (1938–) are brothers and the founders of Pizza Hut. They opened the first Pizza Hut in Wichita in 1958. Today, there are thousands of their restaurants around the world.

Erin Brockovich

George Catlin (1796–1872) was an artist and author who was born in Pennsylvania and specialized in portraits of Native Americans in the western states. He visited more than 140 Native American nations and made more than 500 paintings and sketches of Plains Indians.

Clyde Vernon Cessna (1879–1954) designed his own airplanes. The company he founded with Walter Beech and Lloyd Stearman in 1925 became one of the country's leading airplane manufacturers. He grew up on a farm near Rago.

Walter P. Chrysler (1875–1940) was the founder of the Chrysler Corporation, the third-largest automaker in the United States. He was born in Wamego.

William C. Coleman See page 104.

Glenn Cunningham (1909–1988) was a record-breaking Olympic track star who won a silver medal in the 1,500-meter race in the 1936 Olympics. His nicknames were the Kansas Ironman and the Kansas Flyer. He was born in Atlanta.

John Steuart Curry See page 77.

Charles Curtis See page 93.

George Catlin

Robert "Bob" Dole (1923–) served in the U.S. House of Representatives and the U.S. Senate. He was the Republican nominee for president in 1996. He was born in Russell.

Lewis Lindsay Dyche See page 11.

Amelia Earhart See page 62.

Dwight D. Eisenhower See page 93.

Melissa Etheridge (1961–) is a rock musician and singer who has won Grammy Awards and an Academy Award. She was born in Leavenworth.

Joan Finney (1925–2001) was the first woman governor of Kansas, elected in 1990. Born in Topeka, she graduated from Washburn University in that city, where she studied economic history.

William M. Gallagher (1923–1975) was a photographer who won the 1953 Pulitzer Prize for photography for his photograph of presidential candidate Adlai Stevenson II. He was born in Hiawatha.

Georgia Neese Clark Gray (1898–1995) was the first woman to hold the position of U.S. treasurer, serving from 1949 to 1953. She was born in Richland.

Robert "Bob" Dole

Maurice Greene

Maurice Greene (1974–), nicknamed the Kansas Cannonball, won three gold medals at the World Track and Field Championships in 1999 and two gold medals in the 2000 Olympics. He was born in Kansas City.

Gary Hart (1936–), who was born in Ottawa, served as a U.S. senator from Colorado. He ran for president in 1984 and in 1988. He has written novels under the name John Blackthorn.

Stanley J. Herd (1950–) is an environmental artist who creates artwork with crops, plants, and other natural objects. His work is visible only from the air. He was born on a farm near Protection.

James Butler "Wild Bill" Hickok See page 56.

Dennis Hopper (1936–2010) was an actor, director, painter, and photographer. He was born in Dodge City.

Langston Hughes (1902–1967) was a novelist, poet, and playwright whose works explored African American life. He grew up in Lawrence and Topeka.

William Inge (1913–1973) won a Pulitzer Prize for his play *Picnic* and an Oscar for the film version of his play *Splendor in the Grass*. He was born in Independence.

Eva Jessye (1895–1992), of Coffeyville, was a composer, actor, and singer of African American spirituals. She directed the choir for the first black movie musical, *Hallelujah!*

Don Johnson (1949–) is a film and television actor. He grew up in Wichita and attended the University of Kansas. He won a Golden Globe Award for his role in *Miami Vice* and later starred in *Nash Bridges*.

Walter "Big Train" Johnson (1887–1946) was one of the best pitchers in Major League Baseball history. He was born in Humboldt.

Nancy Landon Kassebaum (1932–) served as a U.S. senator from 1979 to 1997. She was born in Topeka and graduated from the University of Kansas.

Buster Keaton (1895–1966) was a comic silent-film star. His classic movies include *The General* and *Steamboat Bill Jr*. He was born in Piqua.

Mary Elizabeth Lease See page 58.

Jim Lehrer (1934–) is an award-winning television journalist and the former host of *PBS NewsHour*. He has also written novels and plays. He was born in Wichita.

Lutie Lytle (1875–c. 1950), who grew up in Topeka, was one of the first African American women to earn a law degree and the first black woman admitted to the Kansas Bar Association.

Martina McBride

Charlie "Bird" Parker

Edgar Lee Masters (1868–1950) wrote the *Spoon River Anthology*, a series of poems telling the stories of people who lived in a fictional small town. He was born in Garnett.

Martina McBride (1966–) is an award-winning country singer. Her hits include "Wild Angels" and "Valentine." She was born up in Sharon.

Hattie McDaniel (1892–1952), a native of Wichita, was an actress who made dozens of films. In 1940, she won an Academy Award for her role in *Gone with the Wind*, becoming the first African American to win an Oscar.

Oscar Micheaux (1884–1951) was the first African American to produce a feature-length film. He grew up in Great Bend.

Carry Nation (1846–1911) was a member of the temperance movement who protested the drinking and selling of alcohol by destroying Kansas saloons with her cane, stones, bricks, and a hatchet.

Victor Ortiz See page 81.

Charlie "Bird" Parker (1920–1955) was an alto saxophonist, composer, and bandleader. He is considered one of the greatest jazz musicians of all time. He was born in Kansas City.

Gordon Parks See page 78.

Samuel Ramey (1942–) is an opera singer who has made more than 80 recordings, making him the most recorded bass vocalist in history. He was born in Colby.

Damon Runyon (1880–1946) was a sportswriter and short-story writer. The musical *Guys and Dolls* was based on characters in his stories. He was born in Manhattan.

Hattie McDaniel

Jim Ryun

Adolph Rupp (1901–1977) was one of the most successful coaches in the history of college basketball. A graduate of the University of Kansas, he coached the University of Kentucky basketball team for 41 years, leading them to four national championships.

Jim Ryun (1947–) of Wichita was the first high school student to break the four-minute mile. He competed in three Olympic Games and held several world records. He later served in the U.S. House of Representatives.

Gale Sayers (1943–), who was born in Wichita, played football for the University of Kansas Jayhawks. Later, he was running back for the Chicago Bears. He was the youngest player ever elected to the Pro Football Hall of Fame.

Kathleen Sebelius See page 88.

Benjamin "Pap" Singleton See page 55.

Dean Smith (1931–) was born in Emporia. In 1976, he led the U.S. Olympic basketball team to a gold-medal victory. As the legendary coach of the University of North Carolina Tar Heels, he was inducted into the Basketball Hall of Fame in 1983.

Rex Stout (1886–1975) was a mystery writer who grew up in Wakarusa. He wrote more than 40 books about an overweight detective named Nero Wolfe.

Lucy Hobbs Taylor (1833–1910) was the first trained female dentist in the world. She and her husband opened their office in Lawrence.

Vivian Vance (1909–1979) played Ethel Mertz, the best friend of Lucy Ricardo (Lucille Ball's character) in the television show *I Love Lucy*. She was born in Cherryvale.

Mort Walker (1923–) is a comic artist, known for creating two popular comic strips that appear in newspapers: *Beetle Bailey* in 1950 and *Hi and Lois* in 1954. He was born in El Dorado.

Joe Walsh (1947–), born in Wichita, is a songwriter and guitarist who was a member of the rock bands the James Gang and the Eagles.

William Allen White See page 67.

Jess Willard (1881–1968) was the world heavyweight boxing champion from 1915 to 1919. Born in Pottawatomie County and standing 6 feet 7 inches (2 m) tall, he was nicknamed the Pottawatomie Giant.

RESOURCES

BOOKS

Nonfiction

Domnauer, Teresa. *The Lewis & Clark Expedition*. New York: Children's Press, 2013.

Domnauer, Teresa. *Westward Expansion*. New York: Children's Press, 2010.

Hinton, KaaVonia. *Brown v. Board of Education, Topeka, KS, 1954*. Hockessin, Del.: Mitchell Lane, 2010.

LeBoutillier, Nate. *The Story of the Kansas City Royals*. Mankato, Minn.: Creative Education, 2012.

Mara, Wil. *Dwight Eisenhower*. New York: Marshall Cavendish Benchmark, 2011.

Marrin, Albert. *Years of Dust: The Story of the Dust Bowl*. New York: Dutton Children's Books, 2009.

Schraff, Anne E. *John Brown: "We Came to Free the Slaves."* Berkeley Heights, N.J.: Enslow Publishers, 2010.

Fiction

Black, Michelle. *Lightning in a Drought Year*. Frisco, Colo.: Wolf Moon Press, 1999.

Clay, Barry. *The Prairie Adventures of Turk and the Gobblers*. Unionville, N.Y.: Royal Fireworks Press, 1995.

Garretson, Jerri. *The Secret of Whispering Springs*. Sun City Center, Fla.: Ravenstone Press, 2002.

Hubalek, Linda K. *Cultivating Hope: Homesteading on the Great Plains*. Lindsborg, KS: Butterfield Books, 1998.

Jennings, Richard W. *The Great Whale of Kansas*. Boston: Houghton Mifflin, 2001.

Klaassen, Mike. *The Brute*. Port Orchard, WA.: Blue Works, 2005.

Nixon, Joan Lowery. *In the Face of Danger*. New York: Bantam Books, 1988.

Paulsen, Gary. *The Monument*. New York: Delacorte Press, 1991.

Seely, Debra. *Grasslands*. New York: Holiday House, 2002.

Smith, Cynthia Leitich. *Rain Is Not My Indian Name*. New York: HarperCollins, 2001.

Visit this Scholastic Web site for more information on Kansas:
www.factsfornow.scholastic.com
Enter the keyword **Kansas**

INDEX

★ ★ ★

AUTHOR'S TIPS AND SOURCE NOTES

★ ★ ★

While researching this book, I read many excellent books about Kansas. One of the most interesting is *Kansas: A Guide to the Sunflower State*. During the Great Depression, the U.S. government hired writers to create a series of state guides. These books remain valuable sources of information. My copy included a wonderful old map of the rivers, cities, state parks, railroad lines, and even the bus routes of that time.

I consulted other books such as *Kansas: A Bicentennial History*, by Kenneth S. Davis, and *PrairyErth*, by William Least Heat-Moon. I read many children's books about Kansas—and reread *The Wonderful Wizard of Oz*, by L. Frank Baum, just for fun! I also found helpful information in newspapers and magazines such as *National Geographic* and, of course, *KANSAS!* magazine.

In addition, I spent endless hours on the Internet. The governor, the historical society, schools, museums, and even the Kansas Association of Wheat Growers all have Web sites that provide up-to-date information.